Discover LONDON!

JACQUI BAILEY

WELCOME
TO THE BEST CITY
IN THE UNIVERSE!

W
FRANKLIN WATTS
LONDON • SYDNEY

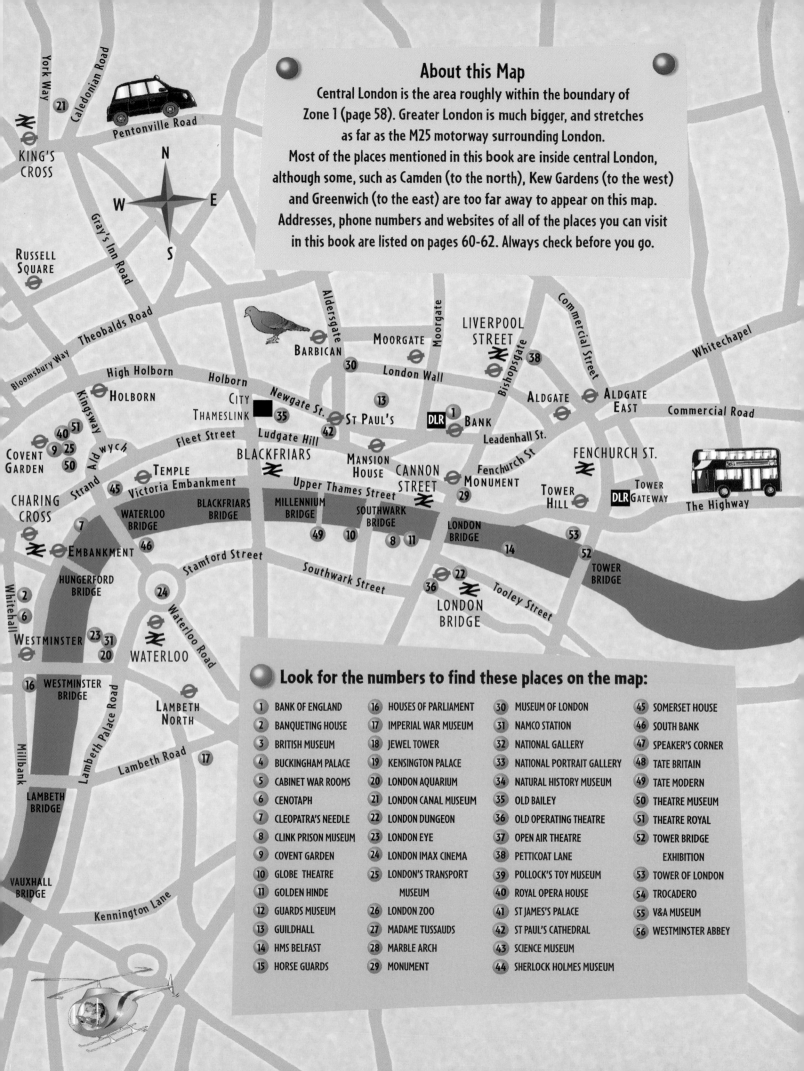

York Way
Caledonian Road
Pentonville Road

21

KING'S
CROSS

N W E S

About this Map

Central London is the area roughly within the boundary of
Zone 1 (page 58). Greater London is much bigger, and stretches
as far as the M25 motorway surrounding London.
Most of the places mentioned in this book are inside central London,
although some, such as Camden (to the north), Kew Gardens (to the west)
and Greenwich (to the east) are too far away to appear on this map.
Addresses, phone numbers and websites of all of the places you can visit
in this book are listed on pages 60-62. Always check before you go.

Gray's Inn Road

RUSSELL
SQUARE

Theobalds Road

Bloomsbury Way

High Holborn
HOLBORN

Holborn

Kingsway

Aldersgate

Moorgate

Commercial Street

Whitechapel

BARBICAN

MOORGATE
Moorgate

LIVERPOOL
STREET

Bishopsgate

ALDGATE

ALDGATE
EAST

Commercial Road

30

London Wall

38

Newgate St.

CITY
THAMESLINK

35

St Paul's

13

DLR 1 Bank

Leadenhall St.

FENCHURCH ST.

40 51

Covent
Garden

9 25

50

Aldwych

Strand

Fleet Street

Ludgate Hill

42

BLACKFRIARS

Mansion
House

CANNON
STREET

Fenchurch St.

Monument

29

Tower
Hill

DLR Tower
Gateway

The Highway

CHARING
CROSS

TEMPLE
Victoria Embankment

45

Upper Thames Street

BLACKFRIARS
BRIDGE

MILLENNIUM
BRIDGE

SOUTHWARK
BRIDGE

LONDON
BRIDGE

53

52

Whitehall

7

EMBANKMENT

WATERLOO
BRIDGE

46

49

10

8 11

14

TOWER
BRIDGE

Stamford Street

Southwark Street

22

36

HUNGERFORD
BRIDGE

24

LONDON
BRIDGE

Tooley Street

2

6

Waterloo Road

23 31

WESTMINSTER

20

WATERLOO

16

WESTMINSTER
BRIDGE

Lambeth Palace Road

LAMBETH
NORTH

Millbank

Lambeth Road

17

LAMBETH
BRIDGE

Kennington Lane

VAUXHALL
BRIDGE

Designed by Matthew Lilly
Illustrated by Jan McCafferty
With thanks to
Stephen Webb and
Transport for London.

First published in 2006 by
Franklin Watts
338 Euston Road
London NW1 3BH

Franklin Watts Australia
Hachette Children's Books
Level 17, 207 Kent Street
Sydney NSW 2000

Created for Franklin Watts by

two's CoMPANY

Copyright © Two's Company 2006

ISBN 0 7496 6489 4

Contents

I ♥ London

I love London. It's big and noisy and full of people, and it is one of the most amazing and wonderful cities in the world. It's not just one city but lots of cities rolled into one. It's an historical city, a royal city, a theatrical city, a fashionable city, a working city and a great city to explore.

London is very spread out. In fact it's mostly a collection of villages that have joined together over the years. Each 'village' and the area around it has its own personality, which is one of the reasons why London is such a varied and exciting city to discover. If you are a new arrival, a visitor, or just someone who wants to read about London, I hope this book helps to give you some idea of what London has in store for you. Have fun!

London is the largest city in Europe. Over 7 million people live in it and more than 300 languages are spoken.

A Short History

AD
50s   The Romans build **Londinium**.
410   The Romans leave Britain and London is abandoned.
700s The Saxons build a town to the west of the Roman city.
890s King Alfred the Great rebuilds London.
1065 Westminster Abbey is built.
1066 William the Conqueror is crowned at Westminster Abbey.
1070s Tower of London is built.
1209 London Bridge is built in stone for the first time.
1348 The first plague kills one-third of all Londoners.
1547 The Houses of Parliament move to Westminster Palace.
1576 London's first theatres open.
1632 The building of Covent Garden begins.
1637 Hyde Park is the first royal park opened to the public.

1649 King Charles I is beheaded at Whitehall Palace.
1665 The last plague strikes London.
1666 The Great Fire of London.
1694 The Bank of England opens.
1698 Most of Whitehall Palace burns to the ground.
1711 The present St Paul's Cathedral is finished.
1750 London's second bridge opens, at Westminster.
1759 The British Museum first opens to the public.
1820s King George IV turns Buckingham House into Buckingham Palace.
1829 The first police force is set up by Robert Peel.

1831 A new London Bridge is built.
1834 Westminster Palace is burnt.
1841 Trafalgar Square is built.
1852 The British Museum moves to its present site.
1861 The government moves its offices to Whitehall.
1863 The first underground train service opens.
1894 Tower Bridge is completed.
1907 The first red buses appear.
1940s Bombing raids on London.
1953 Queen Elizabeth II crowned.
2000 The Millennium Bridge opens.
2002 London celebrates the Queen's Golden Jubilee – her 50th year on the throne.
2012 London hosts the Olympics.

A River Crossing

Almost 2,000 years ago, the invading armies of Ancient Rome landed on the south-east coast of Britain and started to make their way north. They intended to conquer Ancient Britain and make it part of the Roman Empire. Before long, they came to a wide, deep river that stretched from the east coast far inland to the west. They couldn't wade across it and they couldn't go around it. They had to build a bridge.

They followed the river inland until they found a spot where the ground was firm on both sides and the river a little narrower. Here they stopped and built first a bridge and then a settlement.

They called the settlement *Londinium* — today, it is known as LONDON.

> The River Thames is the longest river in England. It flows 338 kilometres from its source near Cirencester (in the Cotswold Hills to the west of England), all the way to the North Sea.

London Bridge

London Bridge has been near the same site since Roman times. The present bridge (below) was built in 1973. Until 1750, central London had only one bridge. Today, there are 18 road bridges, two foot bridges and nine railway bridges over the Thames between Tower Bridge and Richmond Bridge.

Building Bridges

★ For hundreds of years the only other bridge to cross the Thames anywhere near London was Kingston Bridge. The first Kingston Bridge was built of wood in 1219.

★ The second bridge to be built in central London was Westminster Bridge. Completed in 1750, it was rebuilt in 1862. It is painted the same colour green as the benches in the House of Commons.

★ Lambeth Bridge (first built in 1862), to the south of Westminster, is painted the same colour red as the benches in the House of Lords.

★ The prettiest bridge in London is Albert Bridge. Opened in 1873, it looks as if it is made of icing sugar.

LONDON BRIDGE
🚌 BUSES: See page 59
Ⓣ TUBES: London Bridge
⇄ RAIL: London Bridge Station

A Heavy Load

The first London Bridge was built of wood — and then rebuilt time and time again. Finally, in the 1200s a stone bridge with 19 arches was constructed. Its designer, a priest, was buried in a chapel built over the middle of the bridge. By the 1350s there were nearly 200 houses and shops packed on top of the bridge, and the roadway across it was so narrow it was permanently jammed with carts, carriages, horses and pedestrians.

I KNEW I SHOULDN'T HAVE DONE IT!

In the Middle Ages, the heads of traitors were stuck on spikes above the gatehouses at either end of London Bridge. The heads were left there to rot until they fell into the river.

Tower Power

Tower Bridge (below) was built in 1894, when large ships still came upriver. To allow ships to pass under the bridge the roadway was divided in two and a footbridge built above it. Huge weights, hidden in the towers, swing the roadway up out of the way.

Visit the Tower Bridge Exhibition in the north tower.

TOWER BRIDGE
BUSES: See page 59
TUBES: Tower Hill
RAIL: Tower Gateway DLR

THERE ARE NEARLY 300 STEPS TO THE TOP OF THE TOWERS IN TOWER BRIDGE.

YOU MEAN THERE ISN'T AN ESCALATOR?

River Trade

The Romans soon discovered that *Londinium* was the perfect site for a port. Their bridge prevented large ships from going any further upstream so all trading ships had to stop and unload at London. In the 1800s, the port moved to a vast network of docks to east of the city, known as **Docklands** (above). But today's cargo ships are too huge to sail so far upriver, and by 1981 all the London docks were closed.

To find out more about Docklands, take a ride on the Docklands Light Railway (DLR) and visit the Museum in Docklands (page 44).

MUSEUM IN DOCKLANDS
BUSES: See page 59
TUBES: Canary Wharf
RAIL: DLR from Bank or Tower Gateway to West India Quay

Covering Up

For centuries people travelled on the Thames, fished in it, swam in it and drank the water. They also chucked all their sewage into it, and on a warm day it stank! As London grew so did the rubbish, and the smell. Finally, in the mid-1800s, the Victorians built a sewer along the north bank of the river. Smaller sewers fed into this one before they reached the river, and the sewage was carried away downstream. On top of the sewer they built a new road and a series of embankments.

Victoria Embankment stretches from Westminster Bridge to Blackfriars, and is a great place to walk beside the river and see some of the best views of London.

> I WONDER WHAT SHE SEWED WITH THAT?

Cleopatra's Needle

A tall stone monument like a giant finger stands on Victoria Embankment, guarded by a pair of bronze sphinxes. Cleopatra's Needle is thousands of years older than London. It was carved in Ancient Egypt and sent to London in 1819. When it was put on the Embankment in 1878, a time capsule containing Victorian newspapers and photographs was buried beneath it.

Flood Gates

Every now and then the Thames would flood and parts of London would be covered in water. After a bad flood in 1953, people began to look for a way to control tide levels. It took some time to find the answer, but in 1982 the **Thames Barrier** was opened. When its gates are raised they form a steel wall more than half a kilometre long, right across the Thames, stopping the flood water from reaching London.

The Thames Barrier has been used more than 90 times to save London from flooding.

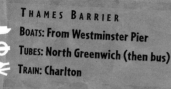

THAMES BARRIER
BOATS: From Westminster Pier
TUBES: North Greenwich (then bus)
TRAIN: Charlton

The Thames Barrier Learning Centre explains how it works. A good way to get there is by riverboat.

The best way to see the Thames is from a boat. Riverboats run daily tours up and down river from Westminster, Charing Cross and Tower Piers.

HMS *Belfast*

HMS *Belfast* is a World War II Royal Navy cruiser, moored on the south side of the Thames not far from London Bridge. She was built in 1936 and was a working ship until 1963, when she was brought to London to become a floating museum.

HMS *Belfast* (below) is a fully-fitted warship. Clamber all over her from top to bottom and find out what life on board was really like.

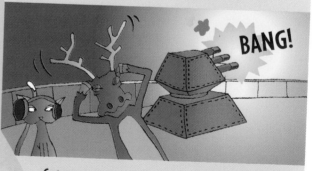

Cats, Rats and Reindeer

BANG!

Cats were part of the crew on HMS *Belfast*. They were kept as pets as well as to get rid of mice and rats.

In 1943, the crew were also given a pet reindeer called Olga. Unfortunately, Olga's life on the ocean waves did not last long. The crew soon discovered that she couldn't stand the sound of gunfire.

City Limits

When the Romans built *Londinium* it was a lot smaller than it is today and they put a wall around it to keep out raiders. The wall was rebuilt many times and for 1,400 years most of London stayed within its boundary, only really bursting out in the 1600s. This walled area was known as the City of London, and it still has that name today. The City has its own laws, its own police force, its own Lord Mayor, and governs itself separately from the rest of London.

The City was always the centre of business and money in London and this has not changed. But today, ultra-modern glass skyscrapers tower over the churches and buildings of earlier times.

The Roman wall was first built in AD 200s, in wood and then in stone. The blocks of stone were brought by river from Kent. The wall was 3.2 kilometres long and as high as a two-storey building. A ditch, 2 metres deep, was dug in front of it.

HOW DO I GET IN?

The Square Mile

The Roman wall stretched from modern-day Blackfriars to the Tower of London (page 30). It covered an area roughly 1 square mile (2.6 square km) — which is why the City is sometimes also called 'the Square Mile'. Roads leading in and out of the City were protected by gatehouses, remembered in the names of some roads and areas in the City today.

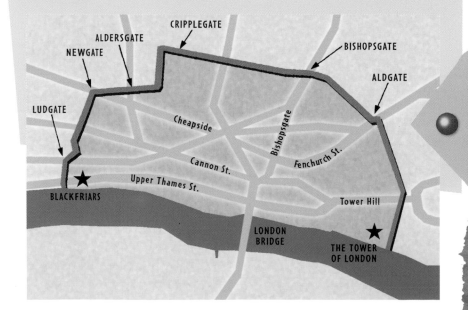

CRIPPLEGATE
ALDERSGATE
NEWGATE
BISHOPSGATE
ALDGATE
LUDGATE
Cheapside
Bishopsgate
Fenchurch St.
Cannon St.
Upper Thames St.
BLACKFRIARS
Tower Hill
LONDON BRIDGE
THE TOWER OF LONDON

London Wall

Parts of the Roman and medieval wall can still be seen. Go to the garden area by Tower Hill tube station, or to the Museum of London (page 44).

LONDON WALL AT TOWER HILL

BUSES: See page 59

TUBES: Tower Hill

RAIL: Fenchurch Street is nearest

The Great Fire!

Sometime after midnight on Sunday 2 September 1666, a fire started in a baker's shop in Pudding Lane near London Bridge. By morning the flames had reached the riverfront and were spreading fast. The fire raged for four days. When it finally ended, more than three-quarters of the City was in ruins, including St Paul's Cathedral. A few years later, a stone tower called the **Monument** was built near to the spot where the fire started as 'a perpetual reminder'.

Get a ticket for the Monument when you visit Tower Bridge (page 7).

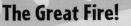

THE MONUMENT

🚌 BUSES: See page 59

🚇 TUBES: Monument, Cannon Street

🚆 RAIL: Cannon Street

Climb the 311 steps to the top of the Monument for some great views of the City.

The Bank of England

The Bank of England was set up in 1694, to lend money to the king and the government, to issue banknotes, and keep stocks of gold and silver bullion (bars). The Bank has been on Threadneedle Street since 1734, although the present building was finished in 1939.

Visit the Bank of England Museum to see its collection of banknotes and gold bars, and even handle a gold bar yourself.

Apparently, in 1836 a sewer-repair man wrote to the directors of the Bank of England to tell them he had discovered a way into their bullion vault through the sewers. He was given a reward of £800.

THE BANK OF ENGLAND

🚌 BUSES: See page 59

🚇 TUBES: Bank, Cannon Street

🚆 RAIL: Cannon Street, Fenchurch Street, Bank DLR

St Paul's Cathedral

The dome of St Paul's Cathedral (below) is one of London's most familiar and well-loved sights. The previous cathedral, 'Old St Paul's', had a spire rather than a dome, but it was destroyed in the Great Fire. The cathedral you see today was designed by the famous London architect, Sir Christopher Wren (who is buried there). It took 35 years to complete and was finally finished in 1710. Today, St Paul's is known as the 'nation's church' and it is where many of the country's important ceremonies take place.

St Paul's is a working church and services are held here every day, but it is also open to visitors.

A Building Site

The first St Paul's was built of wood in AD 604 by Abbot Mellitus, the Bishop of London. It burned down in 675 and was rebuilt ten years later. This second building was destroyed by Vikings in 962 and was then rebuilt in stone. After a fire in 1087, St Paul's was rebuilt again. So many changes were made to the design that this version took more than 200 years to complete, but at least it lasted until the Great Fire in 1666.

The Whispering Gallery is a famous walkway around the inside of St Paul's dome. Its name comes from the fact that a whisper spoken against the wall on one side of the dome can be heard on the opposite side.

ST PAUL'S CATHEDRAL
BUSES: See page 59
TUBES: St Paul's, Mansion House
RAIL: Blackfriars, City Thameslink

An Old Soak

Lots of famous people are buried in St Paul's, including the great seaman Admiral Nelson (1758-1805). Nelson died in battle so his body was soaked in brandy to preserve it. Later, the body and its coffin were put in a lead casket filled with wine. The casket was then put inside two more coffins before being placed in the large black tomb in the Cathedral Crypt.

IT SEEMS SUCH A WASTE.

Merchant Guilds

In the Middle Ages the craftsmen and traders in the City formed groups, called Guilds, to protect their businesses. The Guilds became rich and powerful and controlled most of the running of the City. Each year, the Guilds chose a mayor from among their members and, eventually, the mayor's job became so important he was given the title 'Lord Mayor'.

The 100 Guilds in the City today mainly raise money for charity, but they still meet at the Guildhall in the heart of the City, and they elect the Lord Mayor each year (see Lord Mayor's Show, page 55).

The Guildhall
Parts of the Guildhall date from 1411, making it one of the oldest buildings in London. You can visit it when it is not being used for events.

Old Bailey
London's Central Criminal Court has been at the Old Bailey since 1673. It is named after the street on which it stands. This street follows the line of the western section of the old London wall ('bailey' is an old word for the space in front of a castle or wall). The court grew up here because it was next door to Newgate Prison (page 32). Trials at the Old Bailey are open to the public, but you must be over 14.

DID YOU KNOW THE QUEEN HAS TO ASK THE LORD MAYOR'S PERMISSION TO ENTER THE CITY?

WHAT IF HE SAYS NO?

London now has two mayors: the Lord Mayor of the City of London, who is responsible for just the Square Mile, and the Mayor of London, who is responsible for all of Greater London.

Dick Whittington
The most famous Mayor of London is Dick Whittington. He was a cloth merchant, who was mayor at least three times between 1397 and 1419. According to legend, Dick was a penniless boy who came to London to make his fortune – which he did, after many adventures and helped by his cat. A memorial stone to Whittington and his cat sits on Highgate Hill, where Dick is supposed to have heard the City's bells telling him he would be 'thrice Mayor of London'.

OLD BAILEY
BUSES: See page 59
TUBES: St Paul's, Blackfriars
RAIL: Blackfriars, City Thameslink

A Tale of Two Cities

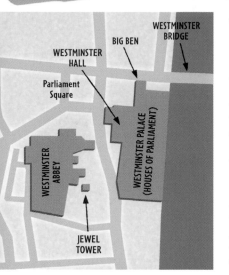

WESTMINSTER BRIDGE

BIG BEN

WESTMINSTER HALL

WESTMINSTER PALACE (HOUSES OF PARLIAMENT)

Parliament Square

WESTMINSTER ABBEY

JEWEL TOWER

The City may be the centre of business and banking in London, but for almost a thousand years it has had to share its power and importance with a rival just a few kilometres upriver – the City of Westminster.

Westminster is the centre of Britain's government, but it owes its position to two other great powers, the Monarchy and the Church.

The Building of a Palace

In the mid-1000s, King Edward the Confessor decided to build a great abbey on the site of an ancient monastery or 'minster'. The minster lay on a small marshy island, to the west of the walled City of London, and was known as Westminster.

Edward was so keen to oversee the building of his abbey that he rebuilt a palace next door to the minster and moved himself and his entire court there. The palace was called the Palace of Westminster. It became the official residence of the king – the place where most of the business of the court was carried out – and it remained so for the next 500 years. Then, in 1512, the palace was damaged by fire and the reigning monarch, Henry VIII, moved out and left it to his advisers: the House of Lords and the House of Commons (page 16).

> THERE MUST HAVE BEEN A LOT OF FIRES IN LONDON IN THE OLD DAYS.

Jewel Tower

The Jewel Tower was built in the 1360s in order to protect the royal treasure. Until the fire at the Palace of Westminster in 1834 (see below), it was actually joined to the palace. Today it is a small museum.

The Palace of Westminster burned down again in 1834, and only Westminster Hall (below) and a few other bits of it survived. Most of the palace that exists today was built between 1840 and 1870. The House of Commons was rebuilt again in the 1940s after a bomb hit it during World War II.

Westminster Abbey

Since it was first completed in 1065, Westminster Abbey (right) has been the favourite church of England's kings and queens. In 1066, the coronations of Harold II and then William the Conqueror took place here, and since then all of England's monarchs (except for two) have been crowned at the Abbey.

Edward's Abbey was rebuilt by Henry III in the 1200s, and Henry VII added more to it a few hundred years later. Today, the Abbey is a working church and a great monument to London's long history.

The Abbey is open to visitors except during services.

The two English monarchs not crowned at the Abbey were Edward V, who died before he had chance to be crowned, and Edward VIII, who gave up the throne before he was crowned.

Fit for a King

The Coronation Chair (left) was built for Edward I and first used by his son Edward II in 1308. It has been used at every coronation since then, even though, in earlier times, a few Abbey schoolboys and others had carved their initials on it!

Queen Elizabeth I is buried in the Abbey, and if you visit the Abbey Museum you can see one of her corsets, along with the death mask of Henry VII, and Admiral Nelson's hat!

Tomb Trail

The Abbey is the perfect place for spotting famous names from history. The first king to be buried there was Edward the Confessor in January 1066, and his massive carved and decorated tomb (right) stands immediately behind the high altar. Lots of other kings and queens are buried here too, along with many poets, writers, musicians and scientists.

After Edward the Confessor's death all sorts of miracles were said to have taken place around his tomb. In 1161 he was made a saint and his tomb is still one of the most sacred places in the Abbey.

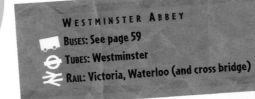

WESTMINSTER ABBEY
BUSES: See page 59
TUBES: Westminster
RAIL: Victoria, Waterloo (and cross bridge)

London Rules!

London is the United Kingdom's capital city — it is the place from which the government rules the country. It is also the official home of the Queen; in the days when kings and queens ruled, the capital was wherever the king and his royal court were. By the Middle Ages, the court had become so big that the king's advisers tended to stay behind when he visited his other palaces. The advisers stayed at the Palace of Westminster and this is where the government and its advisers still meet today, although it is now better known as the **Houses of Parliament**.

The House of Commons has 659 Members of Parliament. Each MP has been chosen to represent a particular part of the country by the people who live there. The political party with the most MPs forms the government, and the head of the party becomes the Prime Minister.

The Houses of Parliament contain nearly 1,200 rooms, 100 staircases and more than 3 kilometres of corridors.

Two Houses in One

The Houses of Parliament are actually divided into three parts. The House of Commons is where the elected Members of Parliament meet to debate issues and agree changes to the laws of the country. The House of Lords is a second debating chamber. Its members are mostly people who have been awarded a title in recognition of their work for the country. Their role is to examine proposals raised by the Commons. And lastly, there are the royal ceremonial rooms: the Robing Room and the Royal Gallery.

UK residents can get tickets to see the Commons in action from their MP, otherwise you can queue for tickets at the St Stephen's entrance. Tours of both Houses are available in the summer.

I COULD TELL THEM HOW TO RUN THE COUNTRY!

HOUSES OF PARLIAMENT
BUSES: See page 59
TUBES: Westminster
RAIL: Victoria, Waterloo and cross bridge

The Opening of Parliament

Each year, in November or after a General Election, the Queen opens a new parliamentary session (year) in a ceremony known as the State Opening of Parliament. The Queen arrives at Parliament in a magnificent royal coach. In the Robing Room, she puts on the state robes and royal crown before entering the House of Lords (below), where she sits on the throne in the Lords' Chamber. The Queen's Messenger, or 'Black Rod', then goes to the House of Commons where he knocks three times on the door to summon MPs to the Lords' Chamber. Afterwards, the Queen reads a speech to both Houses of Parliament.

No king or queen has been inside the House of Commons since Charles I tried to arrest five of its members in 1642.

Big Ben

One of the most famous bits of the Houses of Parliament is the **Clock Tower** (left). The Tower is more than 100 metres high and has 334 spiral steps leading to its top. The four-sided clock at the top of the Tower is sometimes called 'Big Ben', but this is really the name of the bell inside the Tower. Big Ben (the bell) is over 2 metres tall and chimes every quarter of an hour.

IF THE GUARDS SHOW UP NOW I'M IN A LOT OF TROUBLE!

Guy Fawkes

In England, 5 November is known as 'Guy Fawkes Day', 'Firework Night', or even 'Bonfire Night', and is celebrated with fireworks and huge bonfires on which a paper or straw 'guy' is burnt. The reason is that on 5 November 1605, a group of conspirators planned to blow up the king during the State Opening of Parliament. The plot was discovered and one of the conspirators, Guy Fawkes, was found in the cellars beneath the House of Lords with barrels of gunpowder. The conspirators were all executed, but the memory of what they tried to do lives on.

Whitehall

Opposite Westminster Abbey, on the other side of Parliament Square, a broad road leads up towards Trafalgar Square. As many London streets do, this road changes its name about half-way along — it begins as Parliament Street, and then becomes Whitehall. Large imposing buildings line both sides of the road — most of them government buildings. This is where the Treasury is, the Foreign and Commonwealth Office, the Ministry of Defence, the Ministry of Agriculture and the Department of Health.

Chop Off His Head!

On 30 January 1649, Charles I became the only British king to be executed by his own people. After a long and bitter Civil War between Parliament and the King, Charles was finally captured and brought to Parliament where he was found guilty of treason. On the day of his execution, he stepped from a window of the Banqueting House (below – then part of Whitehall Palace) onto a scaffold and was beheaded.

A Vanished Palace

Whitehall gets its name from a vast palace that once sprawled across the road. Originally the home of the Archbishop of York, it was taken over by Henry VIII in 1529. Henry changed its name to Whitehall Palace, and made it his main residence. He turned it into the largest palace in Europe, with over 1,000 apartments, gardens, orchards, and tennis courts. Almost 170 years later, a palace maid was drying some clothing over a charcoal fire and accidentally set fire to the wooden panelling in the room. The fire raged through the palace and most of it burned to the ground. Today, only the **Banqueting House** (left), and the name, Whitehall, survive.

WHITEHALL & DOWNING STREET
BUSES: See page 59
TUBES: Westminster, Charing Cross
RAIL: Charing Cross is nearest

Number 10

Half-way along Whitehall is a very short street called Downing Street, where the Prime Minister lives and works. Number 10 Downing Street has been used by Britain's Prime Ministers since 1732. Not all of them lived there, though. At first, Number 10 was often 'lent out' to friends or family members. It only became established as the PM's home after 1902.

The front of the house looks rather small for such an important building, but Number 10 is much bigger than it seems and is really two houses joined together. Behind the ordinary-looking house in Downing Street is a grand mansion facing onto Horse Guards Parade.

Until the 1900s, Prime Ministers who lived at No. 10 were expected to bring all their own furniture and bedding with them when they moved in.

Horse Guards

The building known as Horse Guards in Whitehall is still the 'official' entrance to St James's and Buckingham Palaces. This is why there are mounted guards on either side of the archway leading through into a large square called Horse Guards Parade. A Changing-of-the-Guard ceremony takes place at the entrance to Horse Guards each morning.

In Memory

Where Parliament Street becomes Whitehall, a stone memorial stands in the middle of the road. This is the **Cenotaph** and it was put here in 1920. Each year on Remembrance Day, the Sunday closest to 11 November, the Queen, members of Parliament, and representatives of the Commonwealth, the Armed Forces and the Churches lay poppy wreaths at the foot of the Cenotaph in honour of those who died in both World Wars.

The Cabinet War Rooms

These are the underground rooms from which Prime Minister Winston Churchill and his War Cabinet worked during World War II. You can visit the rooms and see them as they were when they were in use. In fact the Map Room (above) still has every book, map, pin and notice in exactly the same place as it was on the day after V-J Day, which marked the end of World War II, in August 1945.

THE GLORIOUS DEAD

Royal London

London has been a seat of royal power for more than a thousand years – and has more than its fair share of palaces and royal buildings to prove it. The three major ones, however, are Westminster, St James's and Buckingham Palaces (four if you include Whitehall Palace), because each, at different times, was the main home of the king or queen and the royal court.

The royal court is the name given to the group of people who work directly for a king or queen. Today, the court is more usually known as the Royal Household. It is smaller than it used to be, but it still has about 650 full-time employees.

St James's Palace

St James's Palace (below) was built by Henry VIII in 1532. Henry didn't really need another palace, but he was a great collector of grand houses – he had about sixty of them. After Whitehall Palace burned down, St James's became the official royal residence. William IV was the last king to live there, but members of the royal family have houses or apartments within the palace today, including the Prince of Wales and his sons, who stay in **Clarence House** when they are in London. The State Rooms at St James's are still used for royal ceremonies.

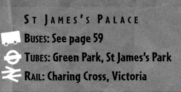

St James's Palace
Buses: See page 59
Tubes: Green Park, St James's Park
Rail: Charing Cross, Victoria

Some of the rooms in Clarence House, which is part of St James's, are open to the public from August to October.

On Guard
Because St James's is a royal palace it is protected by the Royal Guards. One of the best places to get a picture of yourself standing next to a guard is outside the gatehouse to St James's Palace (left) in St James's Street.

Kensington Palace

The Royal Borough of Kensington was once a pretty village on the outskirts of London. In 1689, Queen Mary II bought a house there so that she and her husband William III could escape from Whitehall. The house became Kensington Palace. In 1819, the Duke and Duchess of Kent moved there for the birth of their daughter, the future Queen Victoria. Victoria lived at Kensington until she became queen in 1837. The palace is still a royal residence, and members of the royal family have apartments there.

Parts of Kensington Palace are open to the public, including the rooms where Queen Victoria lived with her mother (above).

KENSINGTON PALACE
BUSES: See page 59
TUBES: High Street Kensington, Queensway or Notting Hill Gate

All Dressed Up

At Kensington Palace you can see a fabulous collection of royal and court dresses and costumes dating from the 1700s to the present day. **The Royal Dress Collection** includes coronation robes, wedding dresses, ball gowns, baby clothes, and uniforms. It also shows some of the dresses worn by Princess Diana, who lived at Kensington Palace from 1981-87.

A Royal Playground

Kensington Palace is surrounded by a beautiful park called **Kensington Gardens**. Designed by Queen Caroline in 1728, the gardens were opened to the public in the 1800s – but only if you looked respectable! Look out for the bronze statue of Peter Pan, the Elfin Oak – a tree-stump carved with fairies, elves and animals – and the Diana, Princess of Wales Memorial Playground (above).

SHIP AHOY, ME HEARTIES!

You can tell when the Queen is at home because a flag flies from the top of the flagpole at the front of the palace.

Buckingham Palace

Buckingham Palace began life as Buckingham House. It was built in the 1700s for the first Duke of Buckingham, but in 1762 the Duke's son sold it to George III who wanted it as a family home. George IV thought it was not grand enough and set about rebuilding it, but the work took so long he died before he could live in it. The next king disliked Buckingham Palace and tried to give it to Parliament, who refused to take it. When Queen Victoria came to the throne in 1837, the palace was still only half-finished. Victoria made more changes, but she and her family did live in it all through her reign, as have all monarchs since.

The State Rooms and some other parts of the palace are open to visitors – see opposite page.

THEY'VE GOT THEIR OWN CINEMA AND SWIMMING POOL IN THERE, YOU KNOW.

A Room with a View

The famous balcony, where the royal family gather to wave at the crowds on special occasions, is right above the central archway at the front of Buckingham Palace. The balcony looks straight out over the huge monument to Queen Victoria and down The Mall.

BUCKINGHAM PALACE

BUSES: See page 59

TUBES: Victoria, Green Park, Hyde Park Corner

RAIL: Victoria

Changing the Guard

Every day from April to July, and every other day for the rest of the year, the ceremony known as the Changing of the Guard takes place in the forecourt of Buckingham Palace between about 10.45 and 11.45 a.m.

The Royal Guards are all professional soldiers and belong to a special division of the British Army called the Household Division. The Household Division is made up of two cavalry (horse) regiments — the Blues and Royals, and the Life Guards — and five foot regiments — the Coldstream Guards, the Grenadier Guards, the Irish Guards, the Scots Guards and the Welsh Guards.

To find out more about the Royal Guards, visit the **Guards Museum** at Wellington Barracks on the west side of the palace. You can see their uniforms, weapons and medals, and even try on a Bearskin Cap.

A State Visit

Buckingham Palace has been open to the public since 1993. In the summer, through August and September, you can visit the 19 State Rooms and part of the palace's 39-acre gardens (left).

The State Rooms are used by the Queen and the royal family to entertain official guests.

The Queen's Gallery

At most times of the year visitors can go to the Queen's Gallery (right) to see paintings, jewellery and furniture from the Royal Collection. The Gallery is on the west side of the palace, and was built on the site of a private royal chapel that was bombed during World War II.

All the Queen's Horses

Between March and October, you can also visit the Royal Mews, where the Queen's cars, coaches and around 30 carriage-horses are kept. The coaches on display include the Gold State Coach (left), which is normally kept for coronations but was used for the Queen's Golden Jubilee in 2002.

Guides dressed in historical costume will take you on a tour of the palace and tell you all about the people who lived there and what they did. They often act out short scenes from history in different parts of the palace.

Hampton Court Palace

A short train ride to the south-west of London, alongside the Thames, takes you to the vast buildings and gardens of Hampton Court Palace (above). This was one of Henry VIII's favourite palaces and he regularly sailed up the Thames to visit it. He brought each of his six wives there, too – in fact some people believe one or two of them still are there (page 40)!

Cardinal Wolsey gave Hampton Court to Henry in 1528. Henry then spent a fortune extending the buildings, but less than 150 years later much of the palace was rebuilt again by William III. Today, only parts of it, such as the central gatehouse, Tudor kitchens and Great Hall date from Henry VIII's time.

You can wander for hours in the Hampton Court gardens, get lost in the Maze, see the oldest tennis court still in use in the world (it was built in the 1620s), and the oldest grape vine that still produces grapes (it was planted in 1768).

The main entrance to the palace, the central gatehouse, once led to Henry VIII's Great House of Easement – a communal lavatory that could be used by 28 people at the same time!

HAMPTON COURT PALACE

RAIL: From Waterloo to Hampton Court Station (journey takes 35 minutes)

BOAT: In the summer you can take a riverboat from Westminster Pier to Hampton Court, but the journey can take up to 4 hours.

IT'S SO BIG IT'S MORE LIKE A VILLAGE THAN A PALACE!

Be prepared to spend the day at Hampton Court if you want to see all of it. The palace buildings spread over 6 acres of ground, and the gardens cover 60 acres.

The Great Kitchen

Henry VIII had a vast household of some 1,200 people, not to mention royal guests and their servants – and they all had to be fed. Henry's kitchens at Hampton Court Palace contained about 50 rooms and 200 kitchen staff. Some of the rooms stored wood, wax candles, linen, spices or nuts. Meat was left to hang in the Flesh Larder, and fish in the Wet Larder. Most of the cooking was done in the three Great Kitchens over six enormous fireplaces. Today, the Great Kitchens are still set up as if to cook a great feast – and if you are lucky you may even find the fireplace lit and the cooks busy at work (right).

Windsor Castle

The other great palace on the outskirts of London is Windsor Castle (left). The Queen regularly stays at Windsor and it is the largest and oldest occupied castle in the world. Windsor Castle was built by William the Conqueror, after 1066, to guard the western road to the capital — it was a day's march from there to the Tower of London (page 30).

Parts of Windsor Castle, including St George's Chapel, are open to the public on most days.

A Royal Burial Place

Lots of royal funerals take place at St George's Chapel in the grounds of Windsor Castle. Ten kings are buried there, including Henry VIII and Charles I.

Windsor Castle was captured by Cromwell during the Civil War and used as a prison. Charles I was held there until his trial and execution in London. Afterwards, Charles's head was sewn back onto his body and he was brought back to St George's Chapel to be buried.

WINDSOR CASTLE
COACH: From Victoria Coach Station, London
Rail: From Waterloo or Paddington Stations to Windsor

Green London

London has lots of parks and green spaces. Some of the largest are the royal parks which were once used only by the king or queen and their court; these days they are open to everyone. Other public parks and gardens once belonged to grand houses, or were built as grassy, tree-lined squares surrounded by houses. Heaths and commons circle central London. In earlier times the main roads into London passed through them, and they were favourite spots for highwaymen to hold up stagecoaches or other passing travellers.

The Diana, Princess of Wales Memorial Fountain is in Hyde Park, and you can follow the circular plaques marking the Princess Diana Memorial Walk. These take you on an 11-km (7-mile) trail through Kensington Gardens, Hyde Park, Green Park and St James's.

Royal Hunting Grounds

There are eight royal parks in and around London. Four of them — **Kensington Gardens** (page 21), **Hyde Park**, **Green Park** and **St James's Park** — stretch across the centre of London from Kensington Palace to Whitehall (page 18).

Hyde Park is the biggest of these four. Henry VIII used it for deer-hunting. Today, there is boating on the Serpentine (below) and, in summer, outdoor swimming and a paddling pool at the Lido. You can cycle and roller-blade on the roads in the park, play tennis at the Sports Centre, or go horse-riding.

If that's too energetic, check out **Speakers' Corner** (near Marble Arch) where anyone and everyone can get up on a soapbox and speak their mind.

Charles I opened Hyde Park to the public in 1637. In 1665, hundreds of Londoners camped out there, hoping to avoid the Great Plague (page 33).

IN WORLD WAR II, PARTS OF HYDE PARK WERE DUG UP AND USED FOR GROWING VEGETABLES.

HYDE PARK
BUSES: See page 59
TUBES: Lancaster Gate, Marble Arch, Hyde Park Corner, Knightsbridge

Green Park

Green Park runs from Hyde Park Corner, alongside Buckingham Palace to the Queen Victoria Memorial at the front of Buckingham Palace. In the Middle Ages, Green Park was a soggy marshland used for burying lepers – people who suffered from an appalling skin disease. Later it was used for hunting deer and sometimes for fighting duels. Now, its broad, shady walks are a favourite place for joggers.

The four other royal parks in and around London are Bushey Park (opposite Hampton Court Palace), Regent's Park (page 28), Greenwich Park and Richmond Park (page 29).

GREEN PARK
BUSES: See page 59
TUBES: Hyde Park Corner, Green Park

WE ARE NOT AMUSED!

St James's Park

When Henry VIII built St James's Palace in 1532 (page 20), he made sure he had enough space for another deer park between it and his palace at Whitehall (page 18). Later, Charles II redesigned the deer park and laid out lawns and avenues of trees. And, even though he liked to walk there himself, he also opened it to the public. There was once an aviary for birds along Birdcage Walk, and both the lake and Duck Island are home to many wild birds, including swans, pelicans and geese.

In summer, free concerts are given at the bandstand in the centre of St James's Park.

Swan Upmanship

In Britain swans are known as royal birds. Since the 1100s all unmarked swans on any public lakes or rivers in the country belong to the Crown. Laws about who could or could not own swans were laid out in the 'Act of Swans' of 1482.

A ceremony called **'Swan Upping'** takes place on the Thames at Windsor in July each year, when all the swans are caught and their markings checked and recorded.

Regent's Park

This was another of Henry VIII's hunting parks until, in the 1800s, the Prince Regent (later George IV) commissioned his architect, John Nash, to turn it into an elegant garden. Regent's Park is a delight. It has a rose garden, bandstand, cafés, three children's playgrounds, a boating lake (with herons and ducks), an open-air theatre in the summer, tennis, golf, acres of grass, and **London Zoo**.

On the north side of the park is the Regent's Canal, where you can walk along the towpath to Camden Lock Market (page 35) or, if you visit the Zoo, you can catch a canal boat.

London Zoo
The north-east corner of Regent's Park has been home to London Zoo since 1828. The Zoo plays an important part in animal conservation and research and helps to protect rare species. It houses about 5,000 animals – everything from giraffes and tigers to anteaters and alligators.

REGENT'S PARK & LONDON ZOO
🚌 BUSES: See page 59
🚇 TUBES: Regent's Park, Great Portland Street, Baker Street

Catch a Canal Boat
Take a trip on a traditional narrow canal boat from Little Venice (near Paddington and Warwick Road tube stations) along the Regent's Canal to Camden Lock Market. Some boats also stop at London Zoo. The trip takes about an hour. To find out more about Regent's Canal visit the **London Canal Museum**.

HAMPSTEAD HEATH
🚌 BUSES: See page 59
🚇 TUBES: Hampstead
🚉 RAIL: Silverlink Metro to Hampstead Heath and Gospel Oak stations

Hampstead Heath
This is a large area of open ground (almost 800 acres) and although it is only 6 km (4 miles) from the centre of London it feels more like country than town. The Heath has woodlands, meadows, hills and 25 ponds and lakes – some of which are open for swimming (all year) and fishing. One of the best views over London is from Parliament Hill (below) on the eastern side of the Heath, and it is also a popular spot for kite-flyers.

I THINK I CAN SEE AUNT MAUD'S HOUSE!

Kew Gardens

Like Hampton Court Palace (page 24), there is so much to see at the Royal Botanic Gardens at Kew that you could spend a whole day there and still not get around all of it. The 300-acre area contains one of the largest collections of plants in the world. In the huge glass Palm House (right), for example, you can see palm trees from all over the world and find out what a tropical rainforest feels like. Or visit the Evolution House and walk through 3,500 years of plant history — look out for the steaming volcano, and the dinosaur footprints. Or you can wander through ten different climate zones in the Princess of Wales Conservatory.

There are also lots of special exhibitions and events at Kew Gardens throughout the year.

The 'Kew Explorer' will take you on a 40-minute bus ride right around the gardens or you can hop off and on at any of the stops along the way.

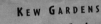

KEW GARDENS
TUBES: Kew Gardens
RAIL: Silverlink Metro to Kew Gardens; or South-West Trains from Waterloo to Kew Bridge

Climbers and Creepers

In Kew's 'Botanical Play Zone' (left), you can 'pollinate' a plant by climbing into it, crawl through an oversized bramble tangle, or get 'eaten' by a giant carnivorous plant.

Richmond Park

This is to the west of London and is the largest London park. It was once a deer park for Richmond Palace. The palace is no longer there, but the park and the deer remain. In 1637, Charles I built a 13-km (8-mile) long wall around the park, and inside it herds of deer still roam freely. The park has woodlands, hills, ponds and grasslands. There are lots of good paths for cycling and roller-blading, plenty of open space for kite-flying, and stables near the park gates if you want to go horse-riding.

From April to September, bikes can be hired in the car park near the Roehampton Gate in Richmond Park.

Bloody London

In AD 61, London was burned to the ground and 70,000 Londoners were slaughtered in an uprising led by Queen Boudicca. Between AD 800 and 1000, Viking raiders tried a number of times to capture or burn the City, and in the Middle Ages plagues killed half of all Londoners. In the 1600s there was the Civil War and the Great Fire, in the 1700s there were riots, and in the 1900s the bombs of World War II. London has survived it all, but the scars of its turbulent past are still there to see.

A Warrior Queen

Near to Westminster Bridge there is a statue of **Queen Boudicca** on her chariot. Boudicca was queen of a British tribe called the Iceni. When her husband the king died, the Romans attacked his wife and daughters and grabbed his wealth. In revenge, Boudicca led an army of warriors against the Romans. At first they were successful, but after the attack on London Boudicca's army was crushed by the Romans and Boudicca poisoned herself. It was after this that the Romans built a stone wall around London.

The Tower of London

After William the Conqueror became king in 1066, he built a square stone fort, called the White Tower, in the south-east corner of the City. He put it there so he could keep an eye on the people of London and watch for enemies coming up the River Thames. Later on, walls, a wide moat, and more towers and buildings were added, and the whole thing became known simply as the Tower.

The Tower (right) was built as a stronghold and a royal palace, but few kings spent much time living there. Instead, it became feared as a royal prison and place of execution.

The White Tower still stands at the heart of the Tower of London, but today it holds a museum rather than prisoners.

A Royal Treasure Store

As well as a prison, the Tower was used as a royal store, particularly for the Crown Jewels. These are the priceless crowns, robes, swords and other objects used at coronations and other royal ceremonies. The Crown Jewels are still kept in the Jewel House at the Tower and are on display. Weapons and armour were stored in the White Tower and exhibits from the Royal Armouries collection can be seen there. Or, if you feel strong enough, visit the Torture Exhibition to find out what happened to some of those unfortunate prisoners.

The Missing Princes

In 1483, Edward V inherited the throne. He was just 12 years old and while he waited for his coronation he and his younger brother were put in the Tower for protection. But instead their uncle Richard III was crowned king, and some time later the two boys mysteriously disappeared. No one knows what happened to them, but almost 200 years later the bones of two children were discovered buried at the foot of a staircase in the Tower.

There have been ravens at the Tower for hundreds of years. There is an ancient belief that the Tower, and the kingdom, will fall if they ever leave it. They are looked after by a special Warder called the Raven Master.

THE LAST PERSON TO BE EXECUTED IN THE TOWER WAS A WORLD WAR II SPY IN 1941.

The Tower Guards

The Tower is looked after by guards called the Yeoman of the Guard and the Yeoman Warders. They are also known as 'Beefeaters' although no one is quite sure why any longer. There are about 40 guards and most live with their families in the Tower. Within the Tower grounds, they have the same powers as the police.

TOWER OF LONDON

BUSES: See page 59

TUBES: Tower Hill

RAIL: Fenchurch Street, Tower Gateway DLR

ENTRY TO THE TRAITORS GATE

The Hanging Tree

Speakers' Corner (page 26) was once the site of the 'Tyburn Tree' — the hanging gallows used for public executions. Between 1196 and 1783, more than 40,000 people died here, many of them for stealing. Hangings were popular events. If a criminal was well known, thousands of people turned up to watch — it was like a carnival. Some of the crowd followed the carts that carried the criminals on their journey from Newgate Prison to the Tyburn. Along the way, the carts would stop at a tavern and the prisoners would be given a last glass of ale (beer).

Today, all that is left of the Tyburn is a small stone plaque (left) on a traffic island at the junction of Edgware Road and Marble Arch.

AH, YES! I SHALL MISS THE LADIES.

One of the most famous highwaymen to be hanged at Tyburn was Claude Duval. Unlike most highwaymen, Duval is said to have been well-mannered and charming, particularly to the ladies he robbed. When he was hanged in 1670, crowds of women came to watch – and weep.

Behind Bars

Until the 1800s, people were sent to prison to wait for their trial rather than as punishment afterwards. Punishment was harsh — you could be hanged for stealing a fancy handkerchief. For lesser crimes you might be fined, publicly flogged, or transported — sent to do hard labour in America or Australia.

Newgate Prison was one of the largest of London's prisons. Even so, it was overcrowded, filthy, stinking and full of disease — many people died before they even got to their trial. Newgate was demolished in 1902 and a new Central Criminal Court, the **Old Bailey** (page 13), was built on top of it.

You can see a full-size reconstruction of some of Newgate's cells (left) in the Museum of London (page 44).

The prisoners in Newgate were given basic food (often raw), but everything else had to be paid for, including cooked food, a bed, bedding, soap and candles. You even had to pay to leave the prison, whether you were guilty or not guilty, and if you died there your body was left to rot until your family paid to take it away.

UH OH, I HOPE THIS IS JUST ACNE!

The Black Death

There were regular outbreaks of plague in London in the Middle Ages. The City streets were full of rubbish, and the poor lived in rat-infested houses. The first plague, called the Black Death, arrived in the south of England in 1348, on two trading ships. It reached London within a few months and killed between 20,000 and 30,000 people.

Over the next 300 years the plague returned again and again. The last, and worst, attack hit London in 1665. This was the Great Plague and it killed more than 70,000 Londoners. Sick people were locked in their homes until they died. Carts collected the dead bodies and took them to be buried in huge plague pits outside the the City.

You can find out more about the plague at the Museum of London's Medieval Gallery (page 44)

A Deadly Bite

The most common form of the plague was bubonic plague. About five or six days after being bitten by an infected flea a blackish blister would appear where the bite was. After this, lumps would swell up around the victim's neck, armpits and groin. Finally, purple-black blotches appeared all over the victim's skin.

The plague was brought to shore by rats from the ships. The rats had fleas and the fleas were infected with plague.

London Dungeon

If you really want to experience the scary side of London's history, visit the London Dungeon. Its exhibits focus on all the gory bits, including torture and execution in Henry VIII's day, the Great Plague, the Great Fire, and the mysterious murderer 'Jack the Ripper'. Not recommended for young children or the faint-hearted!

LONDON DUNGEON
BUSES: See page 59
TUBES: London Bridge, Monument (and cross river)
RAIL: London Bridge

London's Markets

Street markets are fun to visit, even if you don't want to buy anything. Many of London's street markets have existed since the 1600s or even earlier, and sell everything from flowers and fruit to books and furniture. There are local markets in almost every part of London, although most are only open on certain days of the week. Here are a few of the more famous ones.

Covent Garden

Covent Garden should really be called Convent Garden — because that is what it once was. In the Middle Ages, the land belonged to Westminster Abbey and the monks used it for growing their food. In 1670, it became a fruit and vegetable market, and it stayed that way until the 1970s. Then the fruit and veg sellers moved to a large modern market in South London, and Covent Garden's glass-covered market halls (below) were taken over by shops and stalls selling crafts, clothes, jewellery and toys.

The streets surrounding Covent Garden market are also full of interesting clothes and food shops.

Putting on a Show

Surrounded by cafés, restaurants and theatres, Covent Garden is a favourite spot for street performers. On most days you'll find jugglers, acrobats, musicians, puppet shows, and 'living statues' (left) performing in and around the open area called the Piazza. While you are there, you can also drop in and visit the **Theatre Museum** (page 38) and **London's Transport Museum** (page 45).

COVENT GARDEN
🚌 BUSES: See page 59
🚇 TUBES: Covent Garden, Leicester Square
🚆 RAIL: Charing Cross, Waterloo

Camden Lock and Camden Stables Market

Not to be confused with the old Camden Market just off Camden High Street, Camden Lock is a young, lively, hugely popular market that began in the 1970s. It now sprawls out of the lockside buildings into a warren of stalls and small shops crammed into the old canal-horse stables next door. It sells clothes of all sorts, from the latest street fashions to designer knitwear, along with jewellery, leather, books, records, crafts and antiques.

The best time to go is at weekends, when there are often street performers and loads of delicious food stalls. But be warned, it gets fantastically busy.

CAMDEN LOCK MARKET
BUSES: See page 59
TUBES: Camden Town, Chalk Farm
CANAL BOAT: From Little Venice, near Paddington

Portobello Road

This long street (left) rambles down a slight slope from the 'posh end' at Notting Hill Gate to the less-posh end at Ladbroke Grove. Along the way the shops and stalls change from antiques and jewellery to fruit, veg and other foods, and then to second-hand clothes, records, music, street-fashion, and all kinds of other bits and bobs. Shops are open during the week but many stalls are only there on Saturday.

And Then There's ...
- Columbia Road Market, E2. Plants, flowers and gardening stuff of all descriptions. Sunday morning only.

- Greenwich Market, College Approach, SE10. A colourful jumble of old books, coins and furniture, alongside toys, crafts, designer clothes and jewellery. Saturday and Sunday.

Petticoat Lane

This famous 'East End' market (right) is actually in Middlesex Street, E1. The street's name was changed from Petticoat Lane in Victorian times, but the old name, and the market, refused to die. Petticoat Lane sells clothes and shoes of every kind, and has done so since the 1600s. It's busy, noisy and lots of fun. Sunday morning only.

The West End

When London started to spread out in the 1600s, it grew most rapidly in the 'West End' — the gap between Westminster and the City. The area soon filled up with wide streets and grand houses. Before long, the streets around St James's and Piccadilly were lined with shops for the wealthy. By the 1900s, more shops had sprung up — along Oxford Street, Regent Street and Tottenham Court Road. The West End had become the shoppers' paradise it is famous for today.

This statue in the middle of Piccadilly Circus is one of London's most famous landmarks. Originally it was meant to be a 'winged angel of charity', but was later named Eros, after the Greek god of love.

Piccadilly

This street has some of the oldest shops in the West End. Fortnum & Mason – famous for its fantastic food displays – has been on the same site since 1707. Then there's Burlington Arcade (below), where uniformed Beadles still 'keep the peace', as they have since the Arcade opened in 1819. However, if luxury shops aren't for you, there's also the gigantic Virgin Megastore on Piccadilly Circus – packed with every type of music, DVD or game you can imagine.

Regent Street

Running from Piccadilly Circus to Oxford Circus, Regent Street is lined with stores on both sides. About half-way along is Hamleys, one of the largest toys stores in Europe. Hamleys has seven floors and sells everything from pencils to PlayStations. The staff are bouncy and enthusiastic and always have the latest gadgets out on show. It's noisy, chaotic and lots of fun. Further up the street is Liberty, famous for its beautiful fabrics. The main part of the store is built like an old Tudor house, with creaky floors and carved wooden galleries that let you look down to the ground floor. But not everything in Regent Street has been there for centuries. It also has Europe's first Apple Store, where you can try out the latest Apple computers and iPods.

REGENT STREET
🚌 **BUSES:** See page 59
🚇 **TUBES:** Piccadilly Circus, Oxford Circus

Carnaby Street

Off Regent Street, behind Liberty, is Carnaby Street. Once the centre of street fashion during the 'Swinging Sixties', it is now busy reinventing itself. Lots of the shops in Carnaby Street and the small streets leading off it sell clothes, jewellery, bags, boots and sports gear by the latest young designers.

Oxford Street

In the 1700s, Oxford Street (above) was called Tyburn Road and was the route prisoners took to be hanged on the Tyburn Tree (page 32). Today, it is London's busiest shopping street, with over 300 stores, most of them clothes shops or large department stores. The biggest and most famous is Selfridges, which has a large Miss Selfridge section on the ground floor. But there are lots of other well-known names there too, including Nike Town, one of Nike's biggest stores, at Oxford Circus.

I HATE SHOPPING ... UNLESS IT'S FOR ME!

Harrods

London's most famous store of all isn't in the West End, but in Knightsbridge. Harrods (left) is an enormous department store that prides itself on selling just about anything you could ever want to buy. Check out the pet shop, the Egyptian Hall (added after Harrods was bought by the Egyptian millionaire Mohamed Al Fayed), the fantastically ornate food halls and the souvenir department. It's a wonderful shop to look around, though many things in Harrods are quite pricey to buy. You also need to be dressed tidily (no beach shorts or bare tums), or you might be politely asked to leave.

HARRODS
🚌 BUSES: See page 59
🚇 TUBES: Knightsbridge

Theatre Museum

The Theatre Museum in Covent Garden is the perfect place to find out what goes on backstage in a theatre. As well as displays of costumes, stage designs, posters and video recordings, the Museum runs regular workshops, demonstrations and tours. You can put on costumes and stage make-up, talk to professional theatre people, and even have your birthday party in the museum.

London has had theatres since Elizabethan times. Before then, plays were performed in the courtyards of inns. By the 1850s, there were over 20 theatres in and around Covent Garden alone, and music-halls were everywhere. Today, London is world-famous for its theatres and musicals, particularly in the West End and on the South Bank (page 48), although theatres of every description are found all over London.

The longest running play in the world is Agatha Christie's *The Mousetrap*. It has been on stage in London for more than 50 years. You can see it at St Martin's Theatre.

Ballet and Dance

Sadler's Wells in Islington, north London, is the place to go if you love dance. Sadler's Wells and its sister theatre, the **Peacock Theatre** in Kingsway, stage a wide variety of productions from classical ballets such as *Swan Lake*, to family shows and the latest modern dance.

SADLER'S WELLS

🚌 BUSES: See page 59

🚇 TUBES: Angel

🚆 RAIL: King's Cross and Euston are nearest

Theatreland

Many of London's most famous theatres are in the streets around Leicester Square, Covent Garden and the Strand — an area known as 'Theatreland'. One of the oldest is the **Theatre Royal, Drury Lane.** Rebuilt four times, the first Theatre Royal opened in 1663, and the current one in 1812. Nowadays, the Theatre Royal stages some of the biggest musicals in the West End. Just around the corner, in Covent Garden, is the spectacular **Royal Opera House.** The Royal Opera and the Royal Ballet perform here. Tickets are expensive, but popular productions are sometimes shown on giant screens in the Piazza behind the theatre.

There are also daily guided tours around the Royal Opera House, where you can learn about its history and how it works today.

THE PIAZZA'S ALIVE WITH THE SOUND OF OPERA!

The Globe Theatre

Step back in time and see what a theatre was like in Elizabethan times. The Globe (left) is a full-size reconstruction of the original open-air Globe Theatre of 1599, where Shakespeare worked. Sit in the wooden galleries or stand in the yard around the stage and watch Shakespeare's plays performed as they were 400 years ago.

Visit the Globe Exhibition and take a guided tour of the theatre to find out more about an actor's life in Shakespeare's day.

GLOBE THEATRE
Buses: See page 59
Tubes: London Bridge, Mansion House
Rail: London Bridge, Cannon Street

Theatre in the Park

If you like the idea of outdoor theatre, the **Open Air Theatre, Regent's Park** (right) puts on a programme of plays during the summer months – and it can be really magical. The programme usually includes two Shakespeare plays, a musical and a children's play. The theatre serves food and drink, and there are places to picnic. Take a blanket, and an umbrella – just in case!

Children's Theatres

● Plays at **The Little Angel Theatre** in Islington are performed entirely with puppets (left), and there are family workshops to show you how to make and use puppets.

● **The Polka Theatre** in Wimbledon uses puppets, mime, clowns, music and more to create fabulous shows for all ages. They also run drama courses and workshops.

● **The Unicorn Theatre** in Southwark (by Tower Bridge) moved to a fantastic new building in 2005, where they produce a wonderful variety of plays of all sorts and for all ages.

Haunted London

With such a long history behind it, London is bound to have more than its fair share of spooky stories and legends about unhappy ghosts. Here are just a few of London's famous haunted places.

In 1815, a guard patrolling the Tower of London one night said that he saw the shape of an enormous bear loom out of a doorway. Terrified, the guard struck out with his bayonet, only to see the blade pass right through the bear. The guard fainted from fear and died two days later.

Royal Ghosts

Hampton Court Palace (page 24) is fairly full of ghostly goings on. There's Henry VIII's fifth wife, Catherine Howard, who was beheaded. She is said to run along the Haunted Gallery (left) (to plead with Henry for her life) and then return, shrieking. Henry's third wife, Jane Seymour, died at Hampton Court giving birth to his only son, Edward. She is supposed to walk through the Clock Courtyard, carrying a lighted candle. Then there is Edward's nurse, the 'Lady in Grey', who seems to appear in various parts of the palace and has been heard working at her spinning wheel.

The Queen's House

In 1966 an elderly Canadian couple visited the Queen's House (part of Greenwich Maritime Museum, page 43), and took a photograph of the Tulip staircase. At the time, there was no one on the staircase, but when the couple had the photo developed they were amazed to see the ghostly outlines of figures running up the stairs.

COME BACK HERE!

Headless Horrors

So many people were executed in the **Tower of London** (page 30) it's not surprising that some people think a few of them are still hanging around the place. Another of Henry VIII's wives, Anne Boleyn, was beheaded in the Tower and her headless figure is said to drift across the green towards the chapel where she is buried. Henry also had the elderly Countess of Salisbury beheaded at the Tower. She refused to put her head on the block and has apparently been seen being chased by the executioner waving his axe.

Buried by the Bank

The Bank of England (page 11) has been on the same site since 1734 and, although it has been rebuilt a number of times, its past still comes back to haunt it.

In 1812, Sarah Whitehead, the sister of one of the Bank's clerks, was shocked to discover that her beloved brother had been executed for stealing from the Bank. Unable to accept what had happened, she came to the Bank every day for 25 years to ask for her brother. She was such a familiar sight, the clerks called her 'The Bank Nun'. When she died, the Bank paid for her burial in the churchyard that is now the Bank's garden, but they say that she still sometimes appears at the Bank to ask for her brother.

WHAT HAVE YOU DONE WITH MY BROTHER?

I DO WISH SOMEONE WOULD MOVE THIS WALL!

★ The **Original London Walks** company offers guided 'ghost walks' around different parts of London.

Acting Ghostly

The Theatre Royal, Drury Lane (page 38) is supposed to have a very special resident actor, called 'The Man in Grey'. This elegant gentleman in a cloak and riding boots appears in the Upper Circle, where he drifts across the gangway and disappears into the wall. People think he may be the ghost of an actor killed in a stage fight at the theatre in the 1700s.

Visiting No. 10

Even the Prime Minister's house in Downing Street (page 19) is said to have a ghost, or two. People have apparently seen a woman in a long dress and pearls in one of the drawing rooms. And some have said that a little girl sometimes takes the hand of people walking in the basement corridors.

Museums and Galleries

London has loads of museums and art galleries, and there is something for everyone – no matter what you are interested in. Better still, many of them are free. Wherever you go, allow plenty of time. You can spend a whole day in some of the big museums and still not see everything there is to see.

Victoria and Albert Museum (V&A)

The V&A has one of the world's largest collections of art and design – everything from spoons to shoes. The most fun displays are probably the fashion and jewellery, which go back to the 1600s. There are also lots of activities on offer, such as dressing up, or making masks, or using one of the V&A's themed 'Backpack' activity packs with quizzes, games and puzzles.

Natural History Museum

This fantastically carved and decorated building has exhibits on everything from dinosaurs to diamonds. See a full-size blue whale, or get up close to a *Tyrannosaurus Rex* (right). Find out about the history of the human race, what an earthquake feels like, or how a volcano erupts.

You can also get 'hands on' in the Earth Lab.

Science Museum

Check out some real space rockets, and then design your own. Take a trip on the Motionride Simulator, or record your own radio programme.

Find out about the history of medicine (don't miss the shrunken heads), or sit back and see a breathtaking show in the IMAX cinema.

On Science Nights, you can even bring a sleeping bag and camp out here.

The Natural History Museum, Science Museum, and Victoria and Albert Museum were all built on the same street – Exhibition Road in South Kensington.

EXHIBITION ROAD MUSEUMS
BUSES: See page 59
TUBES: South Kensington

The British Museum

This vast museum has exhibits covering every period of human history. Don't miss the Egyptian Rooms, with their fantastic collection of ancient mummies both human and animal (right), coffins and statues. One of my favourite exhibits is a statue of a black cat with earrings! Or explore the king's treasure found in the Sutton Hoo burial ship, or the life and times of Ancient Rome, Africa or Japan.

There are lots of activity trails and activity 'Backpacks' to help you explore the museum, and there are often special family events on offer.

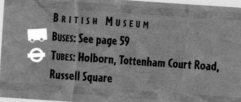

BRITISH MUSEUM
🚌 BUSES: See page 59
🚇 TUBES: Holborn, Tottenham Court Road, Russell Square

Imperial War Museum

This is the best possible place to find out about wars – not just the planes, guns and tanks used in them, but why they happen and what they do to people's lives. There are plenty of tanks, guns and aircraft on show at the IWM, but you can also walk through a full-size model of a trench in World War I, complete with lights, sounds and smells. Or you can sit in a London air-raid shelter and find out what it felt like to be bombed in World War II.

The IWM also has an exhibition on the Holocaust, which tells the story of the persecution of the Jews in World War II.

IMPERIAL WAR MUSEUM
🚌 BUSES: See page 59
🚇 TUBES: Lambeth North, Waterloo, Southwark, Elephant & Castle

Greenwich National Maritime Museum and Royal Observatory

Greenwich is to the east of London, on the Thames. The Royal Observatory is famous for being the home of the 'Prime Meridian' (right), the imaginary line that divides the world into east and west and from which the world's time is measured. The National Maritime Museum is all about the history of British ships, from early canoes to modern naval ships.

While you're in Greenwich, don't forget to visit the **Cutty Sark** – a famous 'tea clipper' sailing ship from the 1800s.

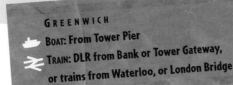

GREENWICH
🚤 BOAT: From Tower Pier
🚉 TRAIN: DLR from Bank or Tower Gateway, or trains from Waterloo, or London Bridge

The Museum of London

The best way to find out about the history of London is to go to the Museum of London. This museum covers everything from prehistoric times, before London existed, up to today. Look out for the oldest skeleton found in London (about 5,500 years old) and discover what ancient people threw into the Thames to please the gods.

There are loads of ancient Roman remains, and models and reconstructions show how Roman Londoners lived. There are clothes, jewellery and swords from the Middle Ages, and you can visit a medieval kitchen. You can also find out about the Black Death (page 33), and watch a model of London burning in the Great Fire (page 11). Or admire the Lord Mayor's golden coach, visit a cell in Newgate Prison (page 32), and walk through a Victorian shopping street.

Pick up a museum fact pack or activity pack to help you explore the exhibits.

MUSEUM OF LONDON
BUSES: See page 59
TUBES: St Paul's, Barbican, Moorgate
RAIL: City Thameslink

Two for One

If you visit the Museum of London, your ticket will also get you into the **Museum in Docklands**. This new museum is worth a trip just to give you an excuse to visit the rebuilt Docklands. The museum tells the story of the Thames – its ports and the people who lived and worked there. There is an interactive children's gallery where you can winch and weigh cargoes, and balance a cargo in a sailing ship. You can see a half-size model of the first stone London Bridge, and visit Sailortown – a dockland street in Victorian times.

The Shepperton woman reconstructed 3640–3100BC

Living London History

Like most museums, the Museum of London runs lots of events alongside their regular galleries, including storytelling, films and workshops. Check their website (page 61) to find out what's on offer. If you click on 'Learning' and 'Kids' you will also find loads of facts about London's history, as well as online games and quizzes to test your knowledge.

I'VE ALWAYS WANTED TO KNOW HOW TO WEAR A TOGA.

The Museum of Childhood is a great place for a day out. Remember to ring ahead or check their website for opening times (page 61).

Museum of Childhood

Part of the Victoria and Albert Museum (page 42), the Museum of Childhood is in Bethnal Green, in the East End of London. It has one of the world's biggest collections of toys, games and children's clothes, dating back to the 1500s. There are all kinds of moving toys, from rocking horses and wind-up toys to train sets through the ages. There are dolls and doll's houses (some of them very grand), puppets, teddy bears, board games and puzzle games.

There are lots of opportunities to play, too. Activity areas include a Punch and Judy theatre, a giant 'snakes and ladders' board, a special 'soft play' area for under-5s, dressing-up, art and drama workshops and storytelling events.

MUSEUM OF CHILDHOOD
- BUSES: See page 59
- TUBES: Bethnal Green
- RAIL: Cambridge Heath, Bethnal Green

Pollock's Toy Museum

If you love old toys and can't get to the Museum of Childhood, this small toy museum is stuffed into two houses in central London. The ground floor is a toy shop, which sells copies of old toys. Above it, the museum has rooms full of mechanical and tin toys, dolls, puppets and toy theatres (above).

POLLOCK'S TOY MUSEUM
- BUSES: See page 59
- TUBES: Goodge Street, Warren Street, Tottenham Court Road
- RAIL: Euston, King's Cross, St Pancras

London's Transport Museum

London's first bus service began operating in 1829. It was a horse-drawn omnibus and to ride in it cost one shilling, which only the wealthy could afford. You can see a full-size model of this first bus in London's Transport Museum, alongside real versions of early motor buses, trams and underground trains — including one of the first Underground railway carriages (known as 'padded cells' because they had no windows).

London's Transport Museum is in Covent Garden. As always, ring ahead or check their website to find out when they are open (page 61).

You can drive an Underground train in a simulator, meet costumed actors who will tell you about the people who made London's transport work, and have fun in the hands-on KidZones.

Looking at Paintings

London has lots of art galleries, but the four biggest are the **National Gallery** and the **National Portrait Gallery** next door, **Tate Modern** and **Tate Britain**. They all have quite different collections and between them cover almost every type of visual art. They all put on lots of special exhibitions, events and workshops.

The Tate Boat runs regular trips between Tate Britain, the London Eye and Tate Modern.

Tate Britain
Tate Britain (above) is on the north bank of the Thames, not far from the Houses of Parliament. It shows the history of British art from 1500 to the present day, including both traditional and modern styles. It has family trails, workshops and events during the holidays.

National Gallery
The National Gallery overlooks Trafalgar Square and is the biggest gallery in London. It has over 2,000 paintings, dating from 1250 to 1900. Many of the paintings are by world-famous artists such as Leonardo da Vinci, Michelangelo, Turner, Constable and Vincent van Gogh.

Louise Bourgeois's MAMAN (1999) installed in the Tate Modern in 2000.

Tate Modern
This gallery is in a converted power station on the south bank of the Thames, across from St Paul's Cathedral. It has displays of modern art and sculpture from all around the world, including pieces by Picasso, Salvador Dali, Jackson Pollock, Andy Warhol and other Pop artists. There are family trails and a children's audio tour.

TATE MODERN
- BUSES: See page 59
- TUBES: Southwark, or Blackfriars on the north bank and walk across the Millennium Bridge

NATIONAL GALLERY & NPG
- BUSES: See page 59
- TUBES: Charing Cross, Embankment, Leicester Sq.
- RAIL: Charing Cross

National Portrait Gallery (NPG)
Behind the National Gallery, the NPG is much smaller and easier to get around. It contains paintings, sculptures and photographs of famous British people, including kings, queens, soldiers, poets, politicians, actors and musicians. Children's trails and activity 'Backpacks' with quizzes, games and puzzles are available.

Just for Fun

There are so many museums, galleries and historic places to visit in London that it can sometimes be a bit overwhelming. But London also has lots of other attractions that are there just for fun (although you can learn interesting stuff, too). Many of them are privately run, however, so tickets can be expensive.

London Eye

This giant wheel (right) was put up on the South Bank of the Thames in 2000, as part of London's Millennium celebrations. Originally, it was meant to be there for five years, but it has proved so popular that it has become a landmark for London, and most Londoners love it.

The Eye is the largest passenger-carrying wheel ever built. It is 135 metres high and turns very slowly, at a speed of 0.26 metres per second. As it turns, the 32 glass and steel passenger capsules are carried around with it, giving their passengers a fantastic view over the Thames and central London. The entire journey takes 30 minutes.

The Eye is run by British Airways, who call each journey a 'flight'. You can queue for flight tickets at the Eye, or book in advance by phone or website.

The London Eye is about 200 times bigger than a bicycle wheel and can carry 15,000 passengers a day.

ON A CLEAR DAY YOU CAN SEE AS FAR AS WINDSOR CASTLE.

I CAN'T, I HAVEN'T GOT MY GLASSES.

LONDON EYE
BUSES: See page 59
TUBES: Waterloo, Embankment, or Westminster and cross bridge
RAIL: Waterloo

Take a Walk on the South Side

It is now possible to walk along almost all of the south bank of the Thames from Westminster Bridge to Tower Bridge. But if that's a bit too far for you, stick to the area known as the **South Bank** (between Westminster and Blackfriars bridges). As well as the pleasure of a tree-lined, traffic-free walk, the South Bank is lined with places to visit, including the Royal Festival Hall, which often has free exhibitions and concerts; the Hayward Gallery; the National Theatre (left) and the National Film Theatre. Finish up at Gabriel's Wharf, where there are cafés, restaurants and craft shops.

Something Fishy

Next door to the London Eye is a large building called **County Hall**. Once home to London County Council, County Hall now contains the **London Aquarium**.

This aquarium is one of the biggest in Europe, with around 3,000 different sea creatures. Enormous salt-water tanks stretch up through two floors, letting you come face-to-face with sharks, rays and all kinds of other ocean fish. You can see how piranha feed, how octopuses change colour and jellyfish float. Shallow touchpools let you get even closer to some small creatures. Aquarium staff give regular talks throughout the day, and you can watch them diving with the sharks in the giant tanks.

The largest tank in the London Aquarium holds 1 million litres of water.

Namco Station

Also in County Hall, Namco Station is a game-players delight. The Arcade section includes the latest video games and simulators. There are seven pool tables, two floors of bowling lanes, and a bumper-car dodgems circuit.

London Imax Cinema

Just the thing for a wet afternoon, the London IMAX Cinema, opposite Waterloo Station, has the biggest screen in the UK. The movies are mostly in 3D and vary from exploring under the oceans to exploring space, or the inside of a haunted castle.

Check the IMAX website to find out what's on (page 61.)

The Imax screen is over 20 metres high – almost as high as five double-decker London buses.

Sailing Away

A full-size working copy of Sir Francis Drake's galleon, the *Golden Hinde* (right) is moored in St Mary Overie Dock by London Bridge. Drake was a favourite of Elizabeth I, and in 1580 he sailed the *Golden Hinde* around the world — the first Englishman to do so. The ship is a living-history museum, with tours, story-telling events, workshops and even overnight stays.

The *Hinde* is sometimes closed for maintenance, so phone before you go to make sure of opening times.

In the Clink

The Clink Prison Museum stands on the site of one of the oldest prisons in England. The original Clink Prison was built in the 1100s and was a working prison until 1780, when it burnt to the ground. Using waxwork models and dark, spooky cells, the Museum gives visitors some idea of what the original prison was like. Exhibits include ball-and-chains, a torture chair and a whipping post, and lots of pictures and information to explain prison life.

CLINK PRISON & GOLDEN HINDE
BUSES: See page 59
TUBES: London Bridge, Monument and cross bridge
RAIL: London Bridge, Cannon Street and cross bridge

Butterflies, Bugs and Other Beasts

Out to the west of London, **Syon Park** has all sorts of attractions. The house and grounds belong to the Duke of Northumberland, and are open to visitors. Also in the grounds is the **London Butterfly House**, where you can walk inside a glasshouse containing hundreds of tropical butterflies. There's the **Aquatic Experience (Tropical Forest)**, where you can see snakes, crocodiles, tortoises, lizards and lots of creepy-crawlies. And if you've still got any energy left, there's a **Snakes and Ladders** adventure playground.

SYON PARK
BUSES: See page 59
TUBES: Gunnersbury
RAIL: Syon Lane via Kew Bridge from Waterloo

What an Operation!

If you have ever wondered what life was like before modern medicine then visit the **Old Operating Theatre Museum & Herb Garret** in the roof space of St Thomas's Church, near London Bridge. The museum was once part of St Thomas's Hospital and the Operating Theatre is laid out just as it would have been in the 1800s (above).

BBC Tours

If you've always wanted to know what goes on behind the scenes at the BBC you can take a tour of the BBC's Television Centre at White City in west London. You have to book tickets in advance, but you are shown around the studios and told how everything works, and you can try things out in an interactive studio.

Sherlock Holmes Museum

For Sherlock Holmes fans, this museum is at 221b Baker Street, which is where Holmes and Watson live in Sir Arthur Conan Doyle's famous books. The rooms in the museum are laid out exactly as described in the books, and visitors are shown around by Holmes's housekeeper.

The Trocadero

Right in the middle of the West End (the entrance is via Piccadilly Circus Underground station), the London Trocadero is a mix of shops, restaurants (Rainforest Café and Planet Hollywood), and entertainment. Funland in the Trocadero has video games and simulators, bumper-car dodgems, pool tables and a bowling alley.

Madame Tussauds and the Planetarium

This popular waxworks museum began in the 1830s by showing wax masks of victims of the French Revolution. Today, it shows life-size and very lifelike wax models (right) of famous people from history and from around the world. Wander through different themed displays, ranging from 400 years of London's history to a truly scary Chamber of Horrors, or a room full of Hollywood stars.

You can get up on stage and play 'air guitar' with your rock heroes, practise your dance moves with Britney, and have your picture taken with the Queen. In the Auditorium (the new-style Planetarium), you can visit the planets, search the stars and explore the mysteries of the universe.

MADAME TUSSAUDS
BUSES: See page 59
TUBES: Baker Street
RAIL: Marylebone

Animal Favourites

If you like animals, don't forget to visit **London Zoo** in Regent's Park (page 28). You can see everything from lions and tigers to pythons and bird-eating spiders. There are always lots of talks and displays going on, and there are animal rides and a petting zoo.

A Day Out at a Theme Park

There are three theme parks within easy reach of London by train (and close to the M25 motorway around London). They are **Legoland Windsor, Thorpe Park,** and **Chessington World of Adventures** (right). Each one offers a slightly different mix of activities, although the main attraction of all of them are the rides — all with different levels of thrill. Legoland is most fun for younger children, for example, while Thorpe Park has the most adventurous rides.

Most of the activities are outdoors, so the parks open in about mid-March and close in September or October.

Just for Birds

The **London Wetland Centre** was created out of an old Victorian reservoir in Barnes, in south-west London. It is now a refuge for water birds and other wildlife. The lakes, ponds and marshes are linked by pathways and bridges, and its glass observatory is just the thing for wet-weather watching. It also has a discovery centre (above) and art gallery.

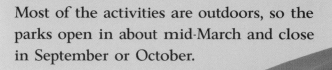
WHICH ONE IS MY PLANE?

RAF MUSEUM LONDON
BUSES: See page 59
TUBES: Colindale
RAIL: Mill Hill Broadway

Royal Air Force Museum

Built on the site of the original London Aerodrome at Hendon, this museum (left) covers the entire history of aviation from hot-air balloons to fighter jets. There are over 100 different aircraft, along with lots of other exhibits, art and photographs. The museum puts on various events during the summer and there is a hands-on interactive gallery where you can find out more about flight and flyers.

Sight Seeing

London isn't all about palaces and old buildings. In the last 50 years lots of new buildings have sprung up, particularly in the City and in Docklands. Many of these buildings have changed the shape of London's skyline. Some are wonderful and some are weird-looking, but they have all become a familiar part of London life.

The Glass Gherkin

The 'Gherkin' is the unofficial name of the building at 30 St Mary Axe in the City. This spectacular glass tower looks as much like a rocket as a pickled cucumber. It is 180 metres high, and uses enough glass to cover five football pitches. Opened in 2004, the building itself is used for offices, but the plaza beneath it has public shops and restaurants.

Tallest Towers

Three of the tallest towers in London are in Canada Square in Docklands (page 8). The tallest of these is One Canada Square (above), also called Canary Wharf Tower, which at 235 metres high is currently the tallest building in London. Numbers 8 Canada Square (HSBC) and 25 Canada Square are both 200 metres high.

BT Tower

From 1965 to 1981 the BT telecommunications tower, just north of Oxford Street, was the tallest building in London. At 191 metres, it is now the 4th tallest. There used to be a revolving restaurant open to the public at the top of the tower, but it was closed after a bomb exploded three floors below it in 1971.

HOW HIGH IS 235 METRES?

AS HIGH AS 53 DOUBLE-DECKER LONDON BUSES.

The 'Wobbly' Bridge

The **Millennium Bridge** (left), linking St Paul's Cathedral on the north side of the river to the Tate Modern on the south side, was the first new Thames bridge in central London for over a hundred years. It opened in June 2000 and almost immediately closed again. So many people walked across it all at once that the bridge began to sway. Instantly nicknamed 'the Wobbly Bridge', it was re-opened in 2002 – but this time with no wobble!

Battersea Power Station

Londoners have a soft spot for this peculiar building (below), on the south bank of the Thames – it looks like an upturned tabletop with its four legs sticking up in the air. The Power Station stopped working in 1982 and was left empty for 20 years. In 2005, work began to transform it into a business, hotel and leisure complex.

Wembley Stadium

The massive new Wembley football stadium in north-west London opened in 2006. It seats 90,000 football fans and cost more than £750 million to build. The Wembley Arch (below) that stands over the stadium is 133 metres high, almost as tall as the London Eye, and can be seen across London.

London City Hall

City Hall (above), where the Mayor of London and the London Assembly work, is on the south side of the Thames, directly opposite the Tower of London. It looks like a lopsided pile of place mats. At its foot is an oval stone amphitheatre called 'The Scoop' which is used for free events in the summer.

London Olympics

London will be hosting the Olympic Games in 2012, and a brand-new 500-acre Olympic Park is being built in Stratford in East London. Other parts of London will be involved in the Olympics too, including the Millennium Dome, Wembley Stadium, Horse Guards Parade and Hyde Park.

The Millennium Dome

The Dome (right) at Greenwich was built for the Millennium exhibition in the year 2000. It is over one kilometre around and 50 metres high and is the biggest enclosed space in the world. The Dome closed in December 2000, but re-opens in 2007 as an entertainment and sports arena.

A London Year

There's always something going on in London at any time of the year. Some events are traditional and date back hundreds of years, and some are fairly new — but they are all part of London's colourful and varied life.

Chinese New Year

Gerrard Street, off Shaftesbury Avenue, is the centre of London's Chinatown. In late January or early February (depending on the year), Chinatown puts on a fantastic parade and festival. Events are free and there are dragon dancers (above), acrobats, theatre and lots of delicious food.

Trooping the Colour

This is one of the biggest royal ceremonies of the year. Held in June, it is the official celebration of the Queen's birthday (her actual birthday is in April). The Guards and Household Cavalry march past the Queen on Horse Guards Parade (page 19) and then escort her back to the Palace. There are marching bands, colourful uniforms, and beautiful horses.

In the evenings, during the week before the Trooping the Colour ceremony, the Royal Guards practise at Horse Guards Parade. It's like a small version of Trooping the Colour, without all the crowds.

The Boat Race

On the Sunday before Easter, or on Easter Sunday itself, teams of rowers from Oxford and Cambridge Universities meet at Putney Bridge for a boat race. The race has been held every year since 1829 and thousands of people turn up to cheer the boats along. The race ends at Chiswick Bridge.

The London Marathon

This event happens around the end of April or early May. The run is 26.2 miles (42 km) long, from Greenwich Park to Buckingham Palace, and over 45,000 people take part, including Olympic champions, celebrities, people in fancy dress and people in wheelchairs. Most run to raise money for charities.

Notting Hill Carnival

Over the holiday weekend at the end of August, the streets around Portobello Road (page 35) in Notting Hill are taken over by a mammoth Caribbean carnival. There are parades, fantastic costumes, dancing, live bands and hundreds of food stalls. Sunday is Children's Day and all the bands and performers on this day are under 21. The main Carnival, and the biggest day, is Monday.

The Lord Mayor's Show

This is held on the second Saturday in November. The Guilds of the City of London (page 13) choose a new Lord Mayor every year, and for the past 800 years the new mayor has paraded through the City on the day he or she takes office. The parade is a huge event, with decorated floats (right), marching bands, fireworks and the Lord Mayor's golden coach.

And Don't Forget ...

- Changing the Guard at Buckingham Palace (page 23).
- Swan Upping on the Thames in July (page 27).
- Guy Fawkes Night on 5 November (page 17).
- The State Opening of Parliament, in November (page 17).

Christmas

From mid-November through December, the streets of London are lit up with Christmas decorations. An enormous Christmas tree is put up in Trafalgar Square (left), and Oxford Street and Regent Street compete with each other for the best street-lighting displays. There are lots of carol-singing services, and traditional pantomimes in the theatres. There is also ice skating at **Somerset House** in the Strand. In December and January, the big square courtyard at Somerset House is turned into an outdoor ice rink (right) surrounded with cafés.

How It Works

These pages are a guide to how London works as a city. They tell you about useful stuff, like finding your way around, catching Tubes (Underground trains), buses, trains, cabs and other information.

Dividing Up London

Londoners use various terms for describing their city. First of all, London is divided by the River Thames, so when people say '**North London**' or '**South London**', they usually mean north or south of the river. (Some North Londoners almost never go South, and vice versa!)

'**Central London**' is anywhere within Zone 1 (page 58) on London's Tube map, and includes '**the City**' (the old walled town); '**the West End**' (the main shopping area around Marble Arch, Tottenham Court Road, Leicester Square and Piccadilly Circus); '**Westminster**' (the Houses of Parliament and Whitehall); and '**the South Bank**' and '**Bankside**' (most of the south bank of the river from Westminster Bridge to Tower Bridge).

The '**East End**' was traditionally a poor area that grew up around the docks to the east of the City. Today, the Docklands area of the East End has been almost totally rebuilt.

London's Boroughs

Officially, Greater London is divided into 32 boroughs, each with its own council, plus the City of London (which runs itself quite separately). But most people talk about the area they live or work in rather than the borough. For example, Bayswater, Knightsbridge and Marylebone are all areas within the borough of Westminster. Underground stations are often named after the area around them.

Cracking the Codes

To find out roughly where in London an address is, look at its postcode. London postcodes are made up of six or seven letters and numbers. The first two or three letters and numbers give you the district. For example, a postcode beginning with WC1 or 2, or EC1, 2, 3 or 4 tells you that the address is in west-central London (Bloomsbury or Covent Garden), or east-central London (parts of Islington or the City).

Then you might have W1 (west), NW1 (north-west), N1 (north), E1 (east), SE1 (south-east), SW1 (south-west). In most cases, the higher the number the further out it is. So the South Bank is in SE1, whereas Greenwich is in SE10.

BAKER STREET W1
CITY OF WESTMINSTER

The Londoner's Bible

The 'London A-Z' is a book of maps that show every street, Tube and railway station in London. Look up a street name in the index (make sure you know the post code) and it will give you a page number and grid reference for the map. Everybody uses it, even people who have lived in London all their lives.

In Britain, the police are also known as 'Bobbies'. The name comes from Sir Robert (Bobby) Peel who organised the first official police force in England – the London Metropolitan Police – in 1829.

A Cross Marks the Spot

Because London is so big, road distances from London are all measured from one spot – the monument known as the Eleanor Cross, in front of Charing Cross railway station.

Queen Eleanor was the wife of Edward I. When she died in 1290, stone 'crosses' were put up to mark the journey of her coffin to Westminster Abbey. This 'Eleanor Cross' is not one of the original ones, though. It was put up in 1865 when the station opened.

Getting Help

Tourist Information Centres (TICs) are great places to get advice about what's on and where to go, and London Transport's **Travel Information Centres** (also TIC) will tell you how to get there. Look out for the TIC sign – a circle or square with the letter 'i' in the middle. Most TICs also sell tickets for theatres, sight-seeing tours and travel, and some exchange foreign money (see page 61 for addresses and websites).

If you get lost, London policemen and policewomen patrol the streets of London on foot and on horseback. They are friendly and helpful, so don't hesitate to ask.

Take a Tour

The easiest and most fun way to get a good view of London is from the top of a double-decker bus – preferably an open-top bus if the weather is good enough. A number of companies run tours. The best ones have guides on board giving live commentaries, and allow you to 'hop on and hop off' at various stops along the way. Two of the biggest tour-bus operators are **The Original London Sightseeing Tour** (right), which runs a Kids' Club tour for 5-12 year olds, and **The Big Bus Company**. Both offer a choice of tours around different parts of London, including all the major sights. **Harrods** also offer a luxury tour, available from their store.

Travelling by Tube

London's Underground system is better known as 'the Tube'. It is one of the busiest travel systems in the world, and carries around 3 million passengers every day. It is usually the quickest and easiest way to get across the city, although you don't see much of London as you travel. Tube trains run from about 5.30 in the morning until after midnight. Try to avoid the 'rush hours', from about 8 to 9.30 in the morning, and 5 to 6.30 in the evening – unless you want to know what it feels like to be a sardine in a hot, packed can!

Map Reading

You can pick up a copy of London's Tube map at most Underground stations and many newsagents. It is all you need to find your way around the Tube system.

There are 12 Tube lines, each shown in a different colour, plus the Docklands Light Railway (DLR):

Bakerloo	Waterloo & City
Central	DLR
Circle	
District	Stations are shown by a small mark on the line.
East London	
Hammersmith & City	Some stations serve more than one line.
Jubilee	
Metropolitan	When lines are linked with a white circle you can change from one to another at this station.
Northern	
Piccadilly	
Victoria	

Travel Info
You can get travel info and maps online and on your mobile phone. Visit the TfL website (page 60), or try the TfL WAP site from your mobile phone. Or, to find the best route from A to B, text TfL on 60835.

TRAVELCARDS ARE COOL!

Ticket to Ride
It is an offence to travel anywhere on London Transport without a proper ticket and there is an immediate fine if you are caught. The simplest and cheapest ticket to get is a 'Travelcard'. A one-day Travelcard, for example, allows you to travel on any Tube, bus, DLR, or overground train within London, as many times as you like in one day. However, you cannot use a one-day Travelcard before 9.30am on a weekday.

In the Zone
The cost of travelling on London's Tubes and buses depends on the number of Zones you want to travel through. London is divided into six roughly circular zones, from Zone 1 in the centre, to Zone 6 on the outskirts. The Zones are shown on the Tube map (see 'Map Reading' above). Before you buy a Travelcard or any other ticket, you need to know which Zone you are travelling from and which Zones you will be going through.

Catching Buses

Buses are cheaper than Tubes and are easy to hop on and off. Traditional London buses are cherry red double-deckers, but today there are many other types of buses in use as well. There are hundreds of bus routes all over London. The best way to find the ones you want is by using bus maps – free from TICs and main travel centres, or from the **Transport for London (TfL)** website (page 60). Inside Zone 1, you may need to have a ticket *before* you board the bus. If you don't have a Travelcard (see 'Ticket to Ride') you must buy a ticket from the machine at the bus stop. On other buses you may pay the driver (board at front), or the conductor (board at back).

Under 16s travel for free on London's buses and trams. You just need to get one of TfL's new smartcards, called an Oyster card, for Under 16s. Pick up a form from any London post office. If you top up your Oyster card at a Tube station you can travel on the Tube with it, too.

KB

BUS STOP

Harrods

towards Hyde Park Corner or Sloane Square

14	74	414
C1	Night Bus N74	Night Bus N97
The Original Tour		

Bus Routes

Bus routes are numbered, and the number and final destination of the bus is always shown at the front and back of the bus (left). Bus stops list the numbers of the buses that stop at them (above) – not all buses stop at every bus stop on a route. At most bus stops there is also a list of all the stops on each route. When the bus you want comes along raise your hand so the driver knows you want to get on the bus.

Black Cabs

The story of London's 'Black Cabs' goes back to the 1600s, when horse-drawn, black hackney carriages first appeared for hire on the streets. Officially, Black Cabs are still called 'hackney carriages' and they are the only taxis that can be stopped and hired on the street. Black Cabs all use the same sort of car (right), but they are not always black any longer and may be all kinds of colours or patterns. When the yellow 'TAXI' light at the front of the cab is 'on' it is available for hire. In order to get a cab licence, Black Cab drivers must show how well they know London by taking a very detailed and difficult test called the 'Knowledge'.

Address Book

Aquatic Experience (Tropical Forest) (p.49)
Syon Park, Brentford, Middx. TW8 8JF
Tel: 020 8847 4730
www.aquatic-experience.org

Bank of England Museum (p.11)
Threadneedle Street, EC2R 8AH
Tel: 020 7601 5545
www.bankofengland.co.uk/museum

Banqueting House (p.18)
Whitehall, SW1A 2ER
Information: 0870 751 5178
www.hrp.org.uk

Big Ben –see Houses of Parliament

Boat Race (p.54)
www.theboatrace.org

British Airways London Eye – see **London Eye**

BBC Tours (p.50)
BBC Television Centre,
Wood Lane, W12 7RJ
Tel: 0870 603 0304
www.bbc.co.uk/tours

British Museum (p.43)
Great Russell Street, WC1B 3DG
Tel: 020 7323 8299
www.thebritishmuseum.ac.uk

Buckingham Palace (p.22)
Buckingham Palace Road, SW1A 1AA
Tickets and information: 020 7766 7300
www.royal.gov.uk (click on 'Art & Residences','The Royal Residences')

Cabinet War Rooms (p.19)
Clive Steps, King Charles Street, SW1A 2AQ
Tel: 020 7930 6961
http://cwr.iwm.org.uk

Canal boat trips (p.28) – see **London Canal Museum** website for list of boat operators

Chessington World of Adventures (p.51)
Chessington, Surrey KT9 2NE
Tel: 0870 999 0045
www.chessington.co.uk

Chinese New Year (p.54)
www.chinatownchinese.com

City Hall (p.53)
The Queen's Walk, SE1 2AA
Tel: 020 7983 4000
www.london.gov.uk

BEFORE YOUR VISIT ALWAYS PHONE OR LOOK ON THE WEBSITE TO CHECK ON OPENING TIMES AND OTHER INFORMATION.

Clarence House (p.20)
Stable Yard, SW1A 1AA
Tel: 020 7766 7303
www.royal.gov.uk (click on 'Art & Residences', 'The Royal Residences')

Clink Prison Museum (p.49)
1 Clink Street, SE1 9DG
Box office tel: 020 7403 0900
www.clink.co.uk

Cutty Sark (p.43)
King William Walk, Greenwich, SE10 9HT
Tel: 020 8858 3445
www.cuttysark.org.uk

Docklands Light Railway (DLR) – see **Transport for London** above

Globe Theatre (p.39)
21 New Globe Walk, SE1 9DT
Tel: 020 7902 1400
www.shakespeares-globe.org

Golden Hinde (p.49)
St Mary Overie Dock, Cathedral Street, SE1 9DG
Tel: 020 7403 0123
www.goldenhinde.co.uk

Guards Museum (p.23)
Wellington Barracks, Birdcage Walk, SW1E 6HQ
Tel: 020 7414 3428

Guildhall (p.13)
Gresham Street, EC2P 2EJ
Tel: 020 7606 3030

Hampstead Heath (p.28)
For details on swimming ponds see www.cityoflondon.gov.uk

Hampton Court Palace (p.24)
East Molesey, Surrey, KT8 9AU
Information: 0870 752 7777
www.hrp.org.uk (historic royal palaces)

Hayward Gallery – see **South Bank and Bankside**

Transport for London
For all information on transport in London, including routes, tickets and the latest travel news, go to the **Transport for London (TfL)** website: www.tfl.gov.uk
or phone: 020 7222 1234
or visit a Travel Information Centre at most main railway stations and Piccadilly Circus.

HMS *Belfast* (p.9)
Morgan's Lane, Tooley Street, SE1 2JH
Tel: 020 7940 6300
www.iwm.org.uk

Houses of Parliament (p.16)
Westminster, SW1A 0AA
Tel: 020 7219 3000
www.parliament.uk

Imperial War Museum (p.43)
Lambeth Road, SE1 6HZ
Tel: 020 7416 5320 / 5321
http://london.iwm.org.uk

Jewel Tower (p.14)
Abingdon Street, SW1P 3JY
Tel: 020 7222 2219

Kensington Palace (p.21)
Kensington Gardens, W8 4PX
Information: 0870 751 5170
www.hrp.org.uk (historic royal palaces)

Kew Gardens (p.29)
Royal Botanic Gardens, Kew, Richmond, Surrey TW9 3AB
Information: 020 8332 5655
www.rbgkew.org.uk

Legoland Windsor (p.51)
Winkfield Road, Windsor, Berks. SL4 4AY
Tel: 0870 504 0404
www.lego.com/legoland/windsor

Little Angel Theatre (p.39)
14 Dagmar Passage, N1 2DN
Box Office: 020 7226 1787
www.littleangeltheatre.com

London Aquarium (p.48)
County Hall,
Westminster Bridge Road, SE1 7PB
Tel: 020 7967 8000
www.londonaquarium.co.uk

London Butterfly House (p.49)
Syon Park, Brentford, Middx. TW8 8JF
Information: 020 8560 7272
www.londonbutterflyhouse.com

London Canal Museum (p.28)
12/13 New Wharf Road, N1 9RT
Tel: 020 7713 0836
www.canalmuseum.org.uk

London Dungeon (p.33)
28-34 Tooley Street, SE1 2SZ
Tel: 020 7403 7221
www.thedungeons.com

London Eye (p.47)
County Hall, Westminster Bridge Road, SE1 7PB
Tel: 0870 5000 600
www.londoneye.com

London IMAX Cinema (p.48)
1 Charlie Chaplin Walk, Waterloo, SE1 8XR
Box Office: 0870 787 2525
www.bfi.org.uk/showing/imax

London Marathon (p.54)
www.london-marathon.co.uk

London Olympics (p.53)
www.london2012.org

London's Transport Museum (p.45)
Covent Garden Piazza, WC2E 7BB
020 7379 6344
www.ltmuseum.co.uk

London Wetland Centre (p.51)
The Wildfowl & Wetlands Trust,
Queen Elizabeth's Walk, SW13 9WT
Tel: 020 8409 4400
www.wwt.org.uk

London Zoo (pp.28 & 50)
Outer Circle, Regent's Park, NW1 4RY
Tel: 020 7722 3333
www.zsl.org/london-zoo

Lord Mayor's Show (p.55)
www.lordmayorsshow.org

Madame Tussauds (p.50)
Marylebone Road, NW1 5LR
Tel: 0870 999 0046
www.madame-tussauds.co.uk

Monument (p.11)
Monument Street, EC3R 8AH
Tel: 020 7626 2717
www.towerbridge.org.uk

Museum in Docklands (p.8)
No. 1 Warehouse, West India Quay,
Hertsmere Road, E14 4AL
Tel: 0870 444 3855
www.museumindocklands.org.uk

Museum of Childhood (p.45)
Cambridge Heath Road, E2 9PA
Information: 020 8980 2415
www.vam.ac.uk/moc

Museum of London (p.44)
London Wall, EC2Y 5HN
Tel: 0870 444 3852
www.museumoflondon.org.uk

Namco Station (p.48)
County Hall, Westminster Bridge Road, SE1 7PB
Tel: 020 7967 1066
www.namcoexperience.com/countyhall

National Film Theatre – see South Bank and
Bankside

National Gallery (p.46)
Trafalgar Square, WC2N 5DN
Tel: 020 7747 2885
www.nationalgallery.org.uk

National Maritime Museum (p.43)
Park Row, Greenwich, SE10 9NF
Information: 020 8312 6565
www.nmm.ac.uk

National Portrait Gallery (p.46)
St Martin's Place, WC2H 0HE
Tel: 020 7306 0055
www.npg.org.uk

National Theatre – see South Bank and Bankside

Natural History Museum (p.42)
Cromwell Road, SW7 5BD
Tel: 020 7942 5000
www.nhm.ac.uk

Old Bailey (p.13)
Central Criminal Court, Old Bailey, EC4M 7EH
Tel: 020 7248 3277
www.oldbaileyonline.org/schools

Old Operating Theatre Museum (p.49)
9a St Thomas's Street, SE1 9RY
Tel: 020 7188 2679
www.thegarret.org.uk

Open Air Theatre Regent's Park (p.39)
Inner Circle, Regent's Park, NW1 4NR
Tel: 020 7935 5756
www.openairtheatre.org

Original London Walks (p.41)
Tel: 020 7624 3978 / 020 7794 1764
www.walks.com

Parks – see Royal Parks website

Peacock Theatre (p.38)
Portugal Street, WC2A 2HT
Box office tel: 0870 737 7737
www.sadlerswells.com

Polka Theatre (p.39)
240 The Broadway, Wimbledon, SW19 1SB
Box Office: 020 8543 4888
www.polkatheatre.com

Open-Top Bus Tours

★ **The Big Bus Company,**
48 Buckingham Palace Road,
SW1W 0RN
Tel: 020 7233 9533
www.bigbus.co.uk

★ **The Original London Sightseeing Tour,** Jews Road, SW18 1TB
Tel: 020 8877 1722
www.theoriginaltour.com

Pollock's Toy Museum (p.45)
1 Scala Street, W1T 2HL
Tel: 020 7636 3452
www.pollockstoymuseum.com

Queen's House, Greenwich –
see **National Maritime Museum**

Royal Air Force Museum (p.51)
Grahame Park Way, NW9 5LL
Tel: 020 8205 2266
www.rafmuseum.org.uk/london

Royal Festival Hall – see **South Bank and Bankside**

Royal Observatory, Greenwich – see **National Maritime Museum**

Royal Opera House (p.38)
Bow Street, Covent Garden, WC2E 9DD
Box office tel: 020 7304 4000
http://info.royaloperahouse.org

Royal Parks (pp.26-27)
www.royalparks.gov.uk

Sadler's Wells (p.38)
Rosebery Avenue, EC1R 4TN
Box office tel: 0870 304 4000
www.sadlerswells.com

St Martin's Theatre (p.38)
West Street, Cambridge Circus, WC2H 9NZ
Box Office: 0870 162 8787
www.vpsmvaudsav.co.uk

St Paul's Cathedral (p.12)
Ludgate Hill, EC4M 8AD
Tel: 020 7236 4128
www.stpauls.co.uk

Science Museum (p.42)
Exhibition Road, SW7 2DD
Tel: 0870 870 4868
www.sciencemuseum.org.uk

Sherlock Holmes Museum (p.50)
221b Baker Street, NW1 6XE
Tel: 020 7738 1269
www.sherlock-holmes.co.uk

Snakes and Ladders (p.49)
Syon Park, Brentford, Middx. TW8 8JF
Tel: 020 8847 0946
www.snakes-and-ladders.co.uk

Somerset House (p.55)
Strand, WC2R 1LA
Tel: 020 7845 4600
www.somerset-house.org.uk

South Bank and Bankside (p.48)
www.southbanklondon.com

Swan Upping (p.27)
www.thamesweb.co.uk (search for 'swan upping')

Syon Park House and Gardens (p.49)
Brentford, Middx. TW8 8JF
Tel: 020 8560 0882
www.syonpark.co.uk

Tate Britain (p.46)
Millbank, SW1P 4RG
Tel: 020 7887 8000
www.tate.org.uk

Tate Modern (p.46)
Bankside, SE1 9TG
Tel: 020 7887 8000
www.tate.org.uk

Thames Barrier Learning Centre (p.9)
Unity Way, Woolwich, SE18 5NJ
Tel: 020 8305 4188
www.environment-agency.gov.uk (search for 'Learning and Information Centre')

Theatre Museum (p.38)
Russell Street, Covent Garden, WC2 7PA
Tel: 020 7943 4700
www.theatremuseum.org.uk

Theatre Royal, Drury Lane (p.38)
Catherine Street, WC2B 5JF
Tel: 020 7494 5000
www.wayahead.com/useful/venues/dru.asp

Thorpe Park (p.51)
Staines Road, Chertsey, Surrey KT16 8PN
Tel: 0870 444 4466
www.thorpepark.co.uk

Tower Bridge Exhibition (p.7)
Tower Bridge, SE1 2UP
Tel: 020 7403 3761
www.towerbridge.org.uk

Tower of London (p.30)
Tower Hill, EC3N 4AB
Information line: 0870 756 6060
www.tower-of-london.org.uk

Trocadero (p.50)
Coventry Street, W1D 7DH
www.londontrocadero.com

Trooping the Colour (p.54)
www.royal.gov.uk (click on Ceremonial Calendar)

Unicorn Theatre (p.39)
147 Tooley Street, SW1 2HZ
Box Office: 0870 053 4534
www.unicorntheatre.com

Victoria and Albert Museum (V&A) (p.42)
Cromwell Road, SW7 2RL
Tel: 020 7942 2000
www.vam.ac.uk

Wembley National Stadium (p.53)
York House, Empire Way, Wembley HA9 0WS
Tel: 020 8795 9000
www.wembleystadium.com

Westminster Abbey (p.15)
Broad Sanctuary, SW1P 3PA
Information Desk: 020 7654 4900
www.westminster-abbey.org

Windsor Castle (p.25)
Windsor, Berkshire, SL4 1NJ
Information: 020 7766 7304
www.royal.gov.uk (click on 'Art & Residences', 'The Royal Residences')

Index

Acknowledgements & Picture Credits

With special thanks to:
Ajay Srivastava from RAF Museum
Amanda Jacobs from Chessington World of Adventures
Amy Burns from The London Dungeon
Andy Begg from BBC Tours
Catherine Worswick from the London Wetland Centre
Charlotte Bond from The Little Angel Theatre
Eddy from Pollocks Toy Museum
Gina Roberts and Jane Rowson from the Environment Agency
Jamie Owen from The Natural History Picture Library
Julie Cochrane from The Museum of London
Kate Binds from the Museum of Childhood
Kirsten Harvey from the Science Museum
Kirsty Chilton from The Old Operating Theatre, Museum & Herb Garret
Libbi Lee from Shakespeare's Globe Theatre
Lucy Murphy from the Churchill Museum
Neil Evans and Sarah Crompton at the National Portrait Gallery
Rocio Riodelaloza and Sue Rolfe from the Theatre Museum, Covent Garden
Simon Harper from Sadlers Wells Theatre
Terry Moore, House of Commons photographer

Top = t, Bottom = b, Right = r, Left = l, Centre = c
p9tr © Environment Agency; p11bl © David Levenson/Alamy; p12 © Fiona Hanson/PA/ EMPICS; p14br © Fiona Hanson/PA/EMPICS; p15cl © The Hoberman Collection/Alamy; p15br © Dean and Chapter of Westminster Abbey; p16 © Terry Moore; p17cr © PA/ EMPICS; p19tr © Martin Keene/PA/EMPICS; p19cr © Imperial War Museum; p21tl & p21cr © Historic Royal Palaces; p21bl © Toby Melville/PA/EMPICS; p22cr © Matt Writtle/PA/ EMPICS; p23tr © Travel-Shots/Alamy; p23cl © 2005 Anwar Hussein/Getty Images; p23cr © Peter Jordan/PA/EMPICS; p23bl © John Giles/PA/EMPICS; p24 © Anna-Marie D'Cruz; p25tr © Historic Royal Palaces; p25c © Aerofilms/Alamy; p29tr & p29cl © RBG Kew – Photos by Andrew McRobb; p29br © Anna-Marie D'Cruz; p30bl © Justin Kase/Alamy; p30cr © Tim Graham/Alamy; p31cr © BlueMoon Stock/Alamy; p32bl © Museum of London; p33b © The London Dungeon; p35tr © Travel-Shots/Alamy; p35cl © David Ball/Alamy; p35b © Network Photographers/Alamy; p38tl © Theatre Museum; p38cl © Morley Von Sternberg; p39tl © Shakespeare's Globe Theatre – Photo by John Tramper; p39c © Alastair Muir; p39bl from The Little Angel's Production of 'The Mouse Queen' – Photo by Adam Crosthwaite; p40c © Historic Royal Palaces; p41 © John Stillwell/PA/EMPICS; p42tr © V&A Images/Victoria and Albert Museum; p42cl © Science Museum; p42cr © The Natural History Museum, London/Kokoro Dreams; p43tr © The British Museum/Heritage-Images; p43cl © Imperial War Museum; p43br © Travel-Shots/Alamy; p44c © Museum of London; p45tr & p45cr © V&A Images/Victoria and Albert Museum; p45cl © Pollocks Toy Museum; p45cr © Transport for London; p46tr © Tate, London 2005; p46cl Louise Bourgeois's MAMAN (1999, steel and marble, 927.1 x 891.5 x 1023.6 cm), installed in the inaugural exhibition of the Tate Modern at Turbine Hall in 2000. Collection of the Artist, courtesy Cheim & Read, New York, photo by Marcus Leith; p46br © National Portrait Gallery, London; p48cr © Christopher Baines/Alamy; p48br © Roy Lawe/Alamy; p49c © The Old Operating Theatre, Museum and Herb Garret; p50tr © Tully Choudry; p50cl © Ernst Wrba/Alamy; p50cb © Madame Tussauds, London; p50br © The Zoological Society of London, 2005; p51tl © Martin Senior; p51tr © Chessington World of Adventures; p51bl © RAF Museum; p53cl © Martin Keene/PA/EMPICS; p53c © Edmond Terakopian/PA/EMPICS; p53br © Jon Arnold Images/Alamy; p54tr © Travel-Shots/Alamy; p54ct © Kirsty Wigglesworth/PA/EMPICS; p54cl © Rebecca Naden/PA/EMPICS; p54cb © Sean Dempsey/PA/EMPICS; p55t © Andy Butterton/PA/EMPICS; p55c © Neil McAllister/ Alamy; p55bl © Peter Jordan/PA/EMPICS; p55br © Michael Crabtree/PA/ EMPICS; p56cb Used with the knowledge and permission of Geographers' A-Z Map Co. Ltd; p60cr © Imperial War Museum; p60br © Andrew McRobb, RBG Kew; p61t Little Angel Theatre, Quentin Blake's 'Angelo' designed by Lyndie Wright. Photo by Adam Crosthwaite; p61c © V&A Images/Victoria and Albert Museum; p61bl © Martin Senior; p62tr © Science Museum; p62cl © Pollocks Toy Museum.
All other photographs © Matthew Lilly.

★